ANTIGONUS II GONATAS

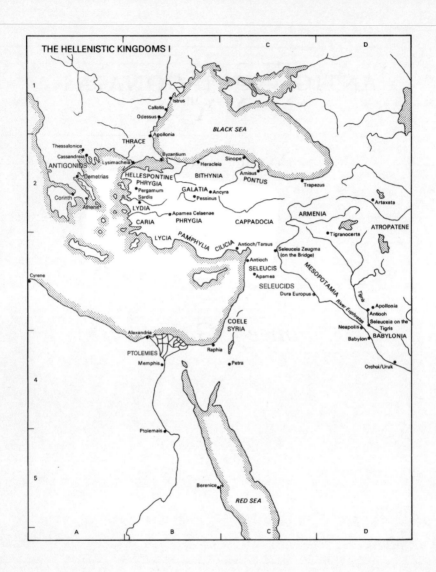

THE HELLENISTIC KINGDOMS I

ANTIGONUS II GONATAS

A Political Biography

Janice J. Gabbert

London and New York

First published 1997
by Routledge
11 New Fetter Lane, London EC4P 4EE

Simultaneously published in the USA and Canada
by Routledge
29 West 35th Street, New York, NY 10001

© 1997 Janice J. Gabbert

Typeset in Garamond by
Ponting–Green Publishing Services, Chesham, Buckinghamshire
Printed and bound in Great Britain by
MacKays of Chatham PLC, Chatham, Kent

British Library Cataloguing in Publication Data
A catalogue record for this book is available from
the British Library

Library of Congress Cataloguing in Publication Data

ISBN 0–415–01899–4

CONTENTS

PREFACE

I have attempted in the following pages to describe the life of an important person in history and the events associated with him. The focus is deliberately narrow; other works exist on the general history of the third century BC and there is no need to duplicate them.

The paucity and ambiguity of the evidence is well known and this is not the place to attempt to solve all problems, even if it were possible. I have, however, attempted to make clear the areas where problems and controversy exist, to indicate possible solutions, and to provide a bibliography for further study of individual problems.

This book was originally to be a joint project with Professor Allen M. Ward of the University of Connecticut. Some progress had already been made when Professor Ward was forced to withdraw due to the pressures of other commitments. I decided to attempt to complete the work alone, but am grateful for his early assistance, and whatever is good in this may be to his credit. Of course, I assume full responsibility for the text in its current condition, including any errors or omissions.

Much gratitude is due also to Richard Stoneman of Routledge for his patience and understanding during the many delays in getting this manuscript into print.

The nature of the subject, and the evidence for it, is such that a biography of Antigonus Gonatas will never be sufficiently complete; the work is never entirely finished. Yet his was an interesting life, in interesting times, of historical importance. It is worth writing about, and I hope it will be found useful.

J.J.G
January 1996

ANTIGONID KINGS OF MACEDONIA

(Dates in brackets are claimed, if not exercised)

(306–301)	Antigonus I and Demetrius I
294–286	Demetrius I Poliorcetes
(286) 276–239	Antigonus II Gonatas
239–229	Demetrius II
229–221	Antigonus III Doson
221–179	Philip V
179–167	Perseus

SELECT CHRONOLOGY

(All dates BC)

1

THE EARLY YEARS

Antigonus Gonatas was born in 319 BC and died in 239 BC. He lived a long life of eighty years and was king of Macedonia, a major power, for half of his long life. The time in which he lived was a period of turbulent transition, full of war and change. Yet it is difficult to know this man, to understand his character; indeed, it is often impossible even to know what he did, still less why, or how, he did it. The evidence is lacking, as is well known.

There are no remaining official archives or records of the king, and there is no surviving narrative of events written by another party, friendly or hostile. The portion of the "universal history" of Diodorus Siculus covering the years after 301 is lost; the narrative of Polybius, where the focus is the rise of Rome, does not begin until 221 BC. The events of the life and reign of Antigonus must largely be interpreted from chance remarks in later sources and randomly surviving contemporary epigraphical evidence, primarily Athenian inscriptions. Inevitably, the evidence from such sources is often ambiguous and the conclusions are controversial. The only prior attempt to describe this man and his times was W.W. Tarn's magisterial work, *Antigonos Gonatas*, published in 1913. That was nearly a century ago. In the intervening years, new evidence has appeared, mostly epigraphical, and new interpretations of events have been suggested. It is time to try again.

Antigonus was probably born in Gonnoi in Thessaly. The name of the town is one possible explanation of his nickname, "Gonatas," which is otherwise not easily explained.[1] It was a likely place for his mother to be: she was Phila, daughter of Antipater, the regent of Macedonia; in 319 BC, Thessaly was firmly under his control. The father of Antigonus was Demetrius, later called "Poliorcetes," who was probably not present at the birth of his first-born (and only

1

GENEALOGY

Antipater + (?)
  children Nicaea, m. Perdiccas (no issue)
           m. Lysimachus, *child* Arsinoë I (m. Ptolemy II),
              Agathocles
     Phila I, m. Craterus, *child* Craterus II
        m. Demetrius I (Poliorcetes)
          children Stratonice (m. Seleucus, Antiochus)
            Antigonus II Gonatas
                m. Phila II (below), *child* Demetrius II
    Eurydice, m. Ptolemy I, *children* Ptolemy Ceraunus,
            Lysandra, Ptolemais
   Cassander m. Thessaloniki (dau. Philip II)
        children Philip, Antipater, Alexander (V) – all
   died young.

       (other children of Antipater)

Antigonus I + Stratonice
  children Philippos (?) died young
    Demetrius I Poliorcetes, m. Phila I, *children* Stratonice I,
            Antigonus II Gonatas
              m. Eurydice of Athens (no issue)
              m. Deidameia (sister of Pyrrhus)
                (no issue)
              m. Lanassa (dau. Agathocles of
                Syracuse) (no issue)
              m. Ptolemais (dau. Ptolemy I) *child*
                Demetrius the Fair
                (. . . *his child* Antigonus Doson)

Lagos + (?(?)) *children* Ptolemy I, Berenice, others
Ptolemy I, m. Eurydice (dau. Antipater): *children* Ptolemy Ceraunus,
           Lysandra, Ptolemais
        m. Berenice (his step-sister?), *children* Arsinoë II, Ptolemy II
        Philadelphus
           Ptolemy II, m. Arsinoë I,
                children Ptolemy III, Lysimachos,
              Berenice (m. Antiochus II)
           m. Arsinoë II (no issue)

Seleucus, m. Apama, *child* Antiochus I
       m. Stratonice I, (dau. Demetrius), *child* Phila II, m.
           Antigonus Gonatas
           Stratonice I m. Antiochus I
           children Antiochus II, Seleucus, Apame, Stratonice II

Lysimachus, m. Nicaea (dau. Antipater), *children*, Arsinoë I and Agathocles
       m. Arsinoë II (dau. Ptolemy I), *children* Ptolemy plus 2 others

legitimate) son, but was with his father, Antigonus I Monophthalmos at his headquarters in Phrygia. Demetrius was only about eighteen years old at the time; he had married Phila at his father's insistence. Monophthalmos thought it was a politically advantageous match, even though Phila was much older than Demetrius. She was probably in her mid- to late twenties, and already a widow (of Craterus) with a young son.

The political marriages which were begun following the death of Alexander continued sporadically for the next few generations. As a result, Antigonus Gonatas was related by blood or marriage or both to just about everyone of political or military consequence in that period. Seleucus I Nikator was at one time or another his brother-in-law and father-in-law; Antiochus, the son of Seleucus, was also his brother-in-law, through the same sister. Ptolemy I Soter was his uncle, Ptolemy II Philadelphus was his cousin, and Pyrrhus, Lysi-machus, and Cassander were also at one time or another his uncles (see the genealogical chart). These multiple marriages were designed to link the families, but often resulted in friction instead.

In this fractious group, the direct line descended from Antigonus I Monophthalmos was unique for the obvious loyalty and dedication to one another. For four generations, no Antigonid was ever murdered, banished, dethroned, or intrigued against by another. Indeed, they usually got along quite well, in different ways and some better than others.

The cross-generational parallels are striking, although perhaps coincidental.

Antigonus I Monophthalmos reached the height of his power and influence late in life; he was over fifty when he became prominent after the death of Alexander. He apparently married late also, had only one wife, and only one son (Demetrius may have had an older brother, who died young). Antigonus I was over forty when Demetrius was born and he indulged the boy, forgiving his childish and adolescent pranks, and bringing him into the family business (power) at an early age. He shared his success with his son: Antigonus was the first of the Successors to take the title of "king" – and it was a joint kingship with his son Demetrius. He lived to be more than eighty years old.

In the same manner, Antigonus II Gonatas reached the height of his power late in life. He had no special position or power until Demetrius died in 283, when Antigonus was already about thirty-seven years old. He, too, married late and only once. He was about forty-two when he married his young niece Phila, by whom he fathered his only legitimate child, his son Demetrius II. He had another son by an Athenian hetaira (Demo), named Halkyoneus, who was born when Antigonus was in his late twenties. Both sons were given considerable fatherly attention, and his legitimate son Demetrius was associated with him in the family business (monarchy) at an early age; Demetrius II was nominally in command of an army against Epirus c. 264 BC, when he was about fourteen years old. Antigonus II also lived a long life: to eighty.

By contrast, both Demetrius I and Demetrius II tasted power at an early age. Both married young and more than once, produced several children and seem to have given little personal attention to any of them. The family tradition of loyalty and affection was real enough, but neither Demetrius played the role of father with any zeal. For example, while both Antigonus I and II took care to associate their young sons in the kingship, Demetrius I was king of Macedonia for nearly seven years, but there is no evidence that he ever named his thirty-year-old son Antigonus joint king. Both Demetrius I and II died young.

Nothing certain is known about the youth of Gonatas. He was not active in his father's power games until he was about twenty-five. For the years before that, we can only surmise the activity or whereabouts of Antigonus by looking at his father's activity, and make some assumptions based on the later attitudes and behavior of Antigonus.

His youth was no doubt spent acquiring the finest education possible. Diogenes Laertius (D.L. 2.110) records that an early teacher of Antigonus was Euphantos of Olynthus, who wrote a treatise for him on governing a kingdom, and he studied with many other philosophers of his time, primarily in Athens. Tarn made much of the fact that Antigonus had been educated in the philosophical schools at Athens, and perhaps he made too much of it. By the late fourth century BC, Athens had already become the "university town" it would remain for centuries. Anyone who could afford advanced education went to Athens if possible. Demetrius certainly provided well for the education of his son, and Athens was a very easy place for Antigonus to be. Antigonus later valued his study with various philosophers, and was known to have remained on friendly terms with many of them: Cleanthes, Menedemos, Bion, Timon of Phlius, Persaios, Arcesilaus, and especially Zeno.[2] Yet many of these friendships, some in fact not very close, seem to date to a much later period. The evidence is anecdotal and inconclusive, but it is possible that many of these friendships, such as they were, were formed after Antigonus became king of Macedonia. During his reign, and at a time when he was over forty years old, he called himself a pupil of Menedemos (D.L. 2.141) and in the context it could be interpreted as polite flattery: not wholly untrue, but not to be taken too seriously. He surely was a student of Zeno the Stoic, either as an adult or earlier in his adolescence. He was genuinely fond of Zeno,[3] and seems to have enjoyed conversing with him. But it would be reaching to assume therefore that Antigonus agreed with Zeno, or became a dedicated Stoic. Indeed, there is evidence to the contrary. On one occasion, Antigonus made a deliberately false statement to Zeno, that his estate had been ravaged by "the enemy" (the incident cannot be dated). He wanted to see Zeno's reaction. As he expected, Zeno was distraught, whereupon Antigonus is said to have remarked, "You see, wealth is not a matter of indifference" (D.L. 7.36). It would seem that the two men had an ongoing disagreement on that subject, and perhaps others. Zeno often complained that Antigonus brought noisy parties to his house (D.L. 7.13); did this mean a few incidents in the youth of Antigonus, or an ongoing amicable irritation? Perhaps Antigonus could consume wine as zealously as his father. The philosopher Bion was known to be on friendly terms with Antigonus (we do not know when), and he was well-known as a heavy drinker (D.L. 4.46). The relationship with Zeno and his circle was long-lasting. It was Antigonus who introduced Persaios to Zeno; Persaios became tutor to Antigonus' son Halkyoneus, and was later sent to Antigonus by Zeno in his stead because Zeno was too old to travel (D.L. 7.36; 7.6). Much later, Persaios was a high-ranking official for Antigonus at Corinth.[4] Much of the anecdotal information about the relationship of Antigonus and philosophers reveals not so much the influence of philosophy on Antigonus, but the political activity of the philosophers. Menedemos of Eretria, also noted for his lively parties, was an envoy to Demetrius, to Ptolemy and to Lysimachus, attempted to intercede with Antigonus regarding affairs in Eretria, moved the decree of Eretria honoring Antigonus after his defeat of the Gauls at Lysimacheia, was a close friend of Antigonus' garrison commander in the Piraeus, and died at the court of Antigonus in voluntary exile (D.L. 2.133–142). The Athenian orator Demochares, never a friend to Antigonus, berated Zeno for his unquestioned influence with Antigonus, an influence Zeno was always careful not to use (D.L. 7.15).

Antigonus' study of philosophy no doubt began in his youth, and continued throughout his life as time and circumstances allowed. He had the opportunity to learn much about statecraft simply by observing the career of his father. The opportunity was even greater to the extent that he shared some of those experiences. It will be useful to review the relevant episodes in the career of Demetrius during the formative years of Antigonus.

Demetrius had had his first military command at the age of about seventeen; he commanded the Companion Cavalry of his father's forces in the battle at Gabene in 317 BC (D.S. 19.40). However, there is no evidence that he introduced his own son to warfare at an equally young age.

Demetrius' first independent command was in 312 at the battle of Gaza, when he was about twenty-five (Plut. *Dem.*. 2; D.S. 19.81, 93); Antigonus would have been an impressionable youngster of about seven years of age.

In his early years Antigonus probably did not spend much time with his father. A very young boy would normally be with his mother, but Antigonus may have remained with his mother well into adolescence because of his father's activities. At least part of his early years were no doubt spent at the court of his grandfather Antigonus I Monophthalmos in Celaenae in Asia Minor, where he would have received his early education and where his father was at least occasionally present. Phila and the twelve-year-old Antigonus were no doubt elsewhere when Demetrius married Eurydice of Athens in 307, and when he took Lamia as his mistress at Cyprus in 306. We do not know where Phila was, or where Antigonus was, although he must have been aware of his father's triumphal entry into Athens, and the great victory over the Ptolemaic fleet off Cyprus. There is no record of the presence of Antigonus at the siege of Rhodes in 305/4, where Demetrius earned the eponym "City Besieger," but since he was already about sixteen, it is not impossible.[5] It is perhaps more likely that the young Antigonus was well into his studies in Athens at this time, and went to Rhodes briefly, if at all.

Antigonus was not likely to have been with his father when Demetrius took yet another wife, Deidameia, the sister of Pyrrhus, in 303 BC (Plut. *Dem.* 25; *Pyrr.* 4). He was also probably not present at the disastrous Battle of Ipsus a year later, although Pyrrhus was.[6] And it was Pyrrhus who was placed in charge of Greece, not Antigonus, when Demetrius sailed to Thrace shortly thereafter (Plut. *Dem.* 31; *Pyrr.* 4). A little later, Antigonus may have joined Phila and

Demetrius in Syria for the betrothal of his sister Stratonike to Seleucus. Phila was then sent on a diplomatic mission to her brother Cassander (Plut. *Dem*. 31–32). Where was Antigonus?

One must wonder at the thoughts of the twenty-year-old Antigonus, observing Pyrrhus, a year younger than he, well-employed by Demetrius and entrusted with considerable responsibility. Yet the subsequent relationship between Antigonus and Pyrrhus, though a constant political rivalry, seems to have involved no personal hostility at all, but rather mutual respect.

And so, in the first twenty years of his life, Antigonus probably heard about his father far more often than he saw him. He heard how his father won military victories; he heard that his father and his grandfather were addressed as kings. He heard about the death of his grandfather and the defeat of Demetrius at the Battle of Ipsus. He knew very well about the warm welcome given to Demetrius by the Athenians, when Demetrius liberated the city from Cassander. Antigonus probably resided in Athens for most of the years between 307 and 301. When news reached the city of the results at Ipsus, Antigonus and everyone else closely associated with Demetrius found it necessary to leave Athens (Plut. *Dem*. 30.3). He had learned what it felt like to be welcomed in Athens, and he now knew how it felt to be unwelcome there.

2

THE APPRENTICE KING

The Athenian insistence that Demetrius, his family, and possessions be removed from Athens after his defeat at Ipsus can easily be explained. There were three reasons: first and most obvious, nobody likes a loser. If the Athenians wanted to stay on good terms with those who were powerful, as I have argued elsewhere,[7] then they would want to avoid any association with someone who had just been decisively defeated by the powerful. Second, Demetrius had not been much help during his recent stay in Athens. Initially, his support of the democracy was very popular and very much appreciated, especially as it was in contrast to Cassander's imposition of the tyranny of Demetrius of Phaleron, who was removed by Demetrius in 307. But Cassander continued to attempt to reassert his control of Athens during the so-called Four Years' War (307–303 BC) in which Demetrius was often absent, as for the naval battle off Salamis in Cyprus (306) and the siege of Rhodes (305/4). Indeed, the Athenians were instrumental in arranging a negotiated end of that siege, precisely because they needed Demetrius back in Athens (Plut. *Dem.* 22–23). Gonatas probably remained in Athens during most of this time, but was too young to be of much help. Various associates and partisans of Demetrius were no doubt helpful, but the Athenians by and large had to fend for themselves against Cassander. There are several references in honorary decrees for Athenians who were active in raising or deploying forces against Cassander (Thymochares of Sphettos, father of Phaidros and Kallias, Demochares, the nephew of Demosthenes, and Olympiodorus).[8]

Finally, Demetrius had long since worn out his welcome in Athens. The period 303/2 was strife-ridden; he still had supporters and sycophants (such as Stratocles, who suggested that Demetrius' words should be considered as coming from the gods), but many were becoming resentful of his increasingly autocratic manner, including his decision to take up residence in the Parthenon with his collection of hetairai, with special honors and perquisites for his favorite, Lamia, the flute-player from Cyprus. It is to this period that the voluntary or involuntary exile of several Athenian politicians must be dated, among them Demochares and the comic poet Philippides (Plut. *Dem.* 24, 27). If he was no help against Cassander, if he was a disgrace and a distraction to political and social life in Athens, and then lost much of his international prestige and power in battle, there was no reason to acquiesce in his continued presence.

The events of the next few years are not well known. Demetrius escaped from Ipsus with 9,000 troops; a great part of his fleet had gone over to Ptolemy, but not all of it. He still possessed garrisons in Corinth, which he had acquired from Cassander in 303 (D.S. 20.103), and probably Megara and Chalkis. No doubt there were other garrisons and supporters in some cities of the Peloponnese where Demetrius had long been active, and he still had friends (and no doubt some mercenaries) in a few cities of Asia Minor. One can guess that Demetrius, Phila, and Antigonus were domiciled primarily in Corinth for the next few years (although Demetrius personally seems never to have stayed in any one place very long). Corinth was the chief base of operations for Demetrius in these years, from which he embarked upon several adventures in the Peloponnesus and in central Greece. It was probably here that father and son first became really acquainted, and during these years that Antigonus gained military experience.

The victors of Ipsus soon had a falling out. Their alliance had not been based on any common interest, but on a common fear of Antigonus Monophthalmos and Demetrius Poliorcetes. With that fear considerably diminished if not removed, they began once again to mistrust one another. It is in this context that another round of marriage alliances was made in an attempt to gain position or influence. In 299 BC, Lysimachus married Ptolemy's daughter Arsinoë, divorcing her aunt Nicaea in the process; his son Agathocles married another daughter of Ptolemy, Lysandra; Seleucus married Demetrius' daughter Stratonike; and Demetrius was betrothed to Ptolemais, daughter of Ptolemy (the marriage was not consummated for several years; she was no doubt quite young).[9] In spite of his defeat at Ipsus, Demetrius was still a force to be reckoned with, and therefore very much a part of the diplomatic maneuverings.

Antigonus, now about twenty or twenty-one years old, may have joined Phila and Demetrius in Syria for the betrothal of his sister Stratonike to Seleucus. Phila was then sent on a diplomatic mission to her brother Cassander (Plut. *Dem.* 31–32). Her mission was to smooth some ruffled feathers; Cassander was not a part of the recent negotiations and marriage alliances, and was not pleased with the opportunistic military adventures of Demetrius in Asia Minor.

The situation in Athens was chaotic. The removal of Demetrius and his associates had not improved the situation at all. Cassander had invaded the Peloponnese while Demetrius was absent for the Ipsus campaign, and it may be this episode which presented a threat to Eleusis and caused Olympiodorus to rally the local population to defeat "the Macedonians" (Paus. 1.26.3). The comic poet Philippides had apparently been resident at the court of Lysimachus since about 303/2; his attempts to get money from Lysimachus for Athens may have begun even before Ipsus; at any rate, by 299/8 Lysimachus had provided large gifts of grain and underwrote some of the costs of the Great Panathenaia of 298 (*I.G.* II², 657). Gifts of money and/or grain to Athens by the powerful kings are often seen as indications of the relationship of Athens to particular kings at that point in time, and rightly so in many instances. One can conclude from this episode that Lysimachus was influential in Athens in the years after Ipsus; on the other hand, Athens was frequently faced with food shortages, often at a crisis level. The need might be urgent to get food into the city as soon as possible, from whatever source. All the hellenistic kings could benefit from the gratitude of Athens, the university town, the polis with a glorious history. At some times, it was worth investing considerable resources for the good will of Athens; at others, perhaps a small amount, if convenient, was in order. It may not be appropriate to draw sweeping conclusions from the evidence of a gift.

The same Philippides had arranged for the burial at his own expense of Athenian casualties at Ipsus. It is worth noting that there were Athenians there: Athens, as a political entity, was not a party in that battle. It should be remembered that, although the kings generally fought their wars with mercenaries, mercenaries could be of any citizenship, and no doubt many Athenians served on all sides. The best known examples are Kallias of Sphettos, the Athenian who spent most of his adult life in the service of Ptolemy (the Kallias decree, Agora I, 7295), and Heracleitus of Athmonon, the Athenian who spent his career in the service of Antigonos Gonatas (*Syll.*³, 454). This fact may explain some apparent shortages of manpower in

Athens; many of the men capable of soldiering had hired out elsewhere.

However great the influence of Lysimachus, Cassander was not yet out of the picture. One of his partisans, Lachares, eventually seized power in Athens under circumstances which are not at all clear. The evidence is a brief mention by Plutarch in his Life of *Demetrius* (33), a brief reference in Pausanias (1.25.7) and the narrative of a very fragmentary papyrus document (*P.Oxy.* XVIII.2082 = *FGrH* 257a). Plutarch merely indicates that Demetrius besieged the city to remove Lachares, after which he acted upon an opportunity to install himself as king of Macedonia. The siege of Athens probably took place in 296/295 BC. The papyrus fragment is in a collection of Olympic victor lists, with which it ends, but not before offering a narrative passage which states that "the generals of the Athenians *estasiasan* [revolted/rose up?]; Charias was the hoplite general and Lachares was in command of mercenaries" and "Charias assaulted the Acropolis . . . *oude epoiese ton demon trephein*" ("but he failed to turn/persuade the demos") and "he [subject unclear] drove off Charias . . . they killed by vote all who fled into the temple, Charias and Peithias and Lysandros son of Kalliphon and Ameinias. Apollodoros made the motion . . . he [subject unclear] besieged those in the Piraeus;" and the document then narrates the death of Cassander and the succession of his sons. The narrative next seems to describe the looting of Athens and melting down of the gold on the statue of Athena by Lachares, which is known from Pausanias, who considered Lachares the most wicked tyrant who ever lived.

At least some of these events seem to precede the death of Cassander in 298/7. The siege by Demetrius was a bitter one; we hear that Epicurus counted out beans to sustain his students since food was so short (D.L. 10.10; Plut. *Dem.* 34). Demetrius could not have maintained such a close siege of the city if he did not control access through the Piraeus. The papyrus document makes reference to hostilities in the Piraeus, and it is probably here that one should place the exploit of Olympiodorus, who was later honored for "rescuing" the Piraeus, among other noteworthy deeds.[10]

Lachares no doubt established a tyranny in the usual fashion, by first becoming popular and persuasive. His relationship with Cassander may have been clear from the beginning and seen as an advantage. If Cassander's friend were in power in Athens, then Cassander might no longer try to regain control of the city and establish an oligarchy or tyranny as before, with Demetrius of

Phaleron. This might seem acceptable, provided that Cassander's friend (Lachares) were not trying to set himself up as tyrant. When he did, fierce opposition arose. The words in the papyrus document imply something very much like civil war. Olympiodorus, who later was supportive of Demetrius, seized the Piraeus from the troops of Lachares, and shortly afterward Demetrius took the opportunity to intervene in the civil war in Athens, assisted by Olympiodorus, who invited him in to the Piraeus.[11] Lachares, while still in control of the assembly, caused a decree to be passed sentencing to death anyone who proposed negotiations with Demetrius. But once he had abandoned hope and fled Athens, the Athenians welcomed Demetrius into the city, and "gave" him the Piraeus and Munychia (which he no doubt already possessed) in gratitude for rescuing them from Lachares. He took the liberty of adding a garrison on the Museum Hill in Athens itself. He also established officials "acceptable to the people" – clearly also acceptable to him (Plut. *Dem.* 34.4). Phaidros of Sphettos continued in office as general *epi ten paraskeuein*; he had been elected to that office for 296/5 and the decree in his honor (*I.G.* II², 682) indicates that he had been elected *twice* in that year. This can only mean that his original election took place under relatively "normal" procedures, but while Lachares was in power. If he had been a fervent partisan of Lachares, it is doubtful that Demetrius would have accepted his continuance in office; in fact, after the successful siege by Demetrius, it is doubtful that the Athenians would have re-elected a man closely associated with one just expelled. The troubles involving Lachares may in fact have been precipitated by the fact that the faction-ridden Athenians had elected to office various officials who were adamantly opposed to each other. The "stasis" of the generals referred to in the papyrus document suggests the armed opposition of Phaidros and Olympiodorus to Lachares, who had also been elected that same year. Demetrius apparently arranged a special election after he entered Athens; Phaidros was again elected to the same office.

Lachares' initial popularity prior to the outbreak of civil war could have lasted from a few months to a year or more. The ensuing civil war may have lasted for many months, perhaps nearly a year. The passage of some considerable time is suggested by Plutarch's account (*Dem.* 33, 34) which, although very summary in nature, places several time-consuming events between the initial decision of Demetrius to intervene and his actual siege of the city. He was in Asia when he learned of the trouble involving Lachares. He made ready and sailed for Athens. His fleet encountered a severe storm (winter?) and he suffered heavy losses of ships and manpower. He began military activities in Attica, which were ineffective; he then sent word to Asia to dispatch another fleet, and while waiting for its arrival he campaigned in the Peloponnese to improve or shore up his positions there (no details are available). During one encounter, he was wounded by a javelin bolt to his jaw. After he recovered from this wound, he continued to campaign, successfully, against some Peloponnesian cities which had become disaffected. He marched to Eleusis and Rhamnous in Attica and gained control of those fortresses. A Ptolemaic fleet was seen off Aegina, near Athens, but at that point his fleet of 300 ships had arrived and the Ptolemaic fleet withdrew. It is at that point that he began the siege of Athens. This probably did not exceed a year in duration; in view of the chronic shortages of food in Athens, the city could be starved into submission within a relatively short period – providing, of course, that the blockade was complete and the Piraeus was not available to the Athenians, as is apparent in this instance.

It was during this general time that Demetrius received some unsettling news: Lysimachus had taken control of some of his Asian possessions; Ptolemy had taken most of Cyprus except for the city of Salamis, and his mother and children, then resident in Cyprus, had been captured (they were well-treated by Ptolemy and later released). There is no mention of his wife, or wives. It is interesting to note that his mother, Stratonike, still lived. The children mentioned cannot be the children of Phila: Antigonus Gonatas was already about twenty-five years old, and his sister Stratonike was already married to Seleucus. Demetrius had not yet consummated his marriage to Ptolemais, nor yet married Lanassa, and so these must be children of Deidameia, now dead, or less likely, Eurydice of Athens, whom he had married in 306 – or other illegitimate children whose mother is unknown.

Antigonus was certainly present at the siege of Athens in 295 BC, which resulted in a firm control of the city by Demetrius. The eponymous archon of Athens was normally selected by lot, but the archon for 294/3, and again for 293/2, was Olympiodorus (*I.G.* II², 689, 349). Directly or indirectly, Demetrius was appointing the archons. He shortly thereafter succeeded in making himself king in Macedonia (by murdering Alexander, the surviving son of Cassander). At this time, Antigonus was serving in his father's army (Plut.

13

Dem. 37.3); he must have been about twenty-five, although Plutarch refers to him as a *meirakion*, a "youth."

Perhaps a year later, he was placed in charge of Boeotia by Demetrius; during the campaign in Boeotia, Antigonus won at least one battle and conducted at least one siege, in full command, without the presence of Demetrius. Plutarch's summary of these events (*Dem.* 39) is naturally lacking detail: Demetrius had initially established friendly relations with the Boeotians, but at the instigation of the Spartan exile Cleonymus the Thebans "revolted," Demetrius brought up siege engines, Cleonymus withdrew and the Thebans surrendered. Demetrius exacted tribute, installed garrisons, and placed Hieronymus of Cardia in charge as an overseer of affairs. All of that didn't seem to do much good. Demetrius traveled with his army (an army?) to Thrace to take advantage of the apparent absence of Lysimachus (who returned too quickly) and in his absence the Boeotians revolted again. He quickly turned back to Boeotia, to find that his son Antigonus had already defeated the Boeotians in battle. At this point Pyrrhus invaded Thessaly. Demetrius went north to engage him, leaving Antigonus in charge of the siege of Thebes. Pyrrhus retreated and Demetrius returned to Thebes. Although Antigonus may have been able (or expected) to rely on the guidance of the more experienced Hieronymus, it seems that in these actions he was acting on his own, and was expected to be capable of looking after the interests of Demetrius. Hieronymus, in any case, was not known for his military successes; his talents were more in the political arena. This reference in Plutarch (*Dem.* 37–39) is the earliest reference to any military activity on the part of Antigonus Gonatas. That he was still learning is perhaps reflected in an anecdote told by Plutarch (*Dem.* 40): Demetrius had undertaken a rigorous siege of the city of Thebes, in company with his son Antigonus, and Antigonus questioned the apparently unnecessary casualties. Demetrius was angered to have his tactics questioned, and retorted with something equivalent to "what do you care?" But he nevertheless altered his tactics somewhat and treated the city once taken with considerable leniency. The episode reveals that Demetrius was not quite ready to consider his son an equal, but he was ready and willing to listen to him; it also indicates that the Antigonid tradition of cooperation between father and son, established by the elder Antigonus with Demetrius, would continue. By *c.* 295, at the age of about twenty-five, Antigonus had come into his own. He was the son and heir-apparent of the king of Macedonia; it would never be otherwise.

The initial popularity of Demetrius in Macedonia was probably due more to the reputation of his wife, the noble Phila, daughter of Antipater, than to his own flamboyant character, which made him popular with the troops. Hostile sources (there are no other kind) insist that he was not a competent governor. Antigonus could learn from this, too. Antigonus, by character or intent, was not an especially colorful character, and his chief public virtues were competence and efficiency.

It seems consistent with the evidence to suggest that when Demetrius was King of Macedonia from 295 to 287 BC, he spent much of his time in Macedonia and in his newly founded city of Demetrias in Thessaly, and relatively little in Athens, while Antigonus spent more time in Athens and less in Macedonia. Later sources are hostile to both kings, but for different reasons. The general picture of Demetrius is one of an incompetent king who lacked the patience to govern properly and was often impulsive in his dealings with others. The criticism of Antigonus Gonatas, on the other hand, has nothing to do with incompetence in Macedonia (indeed, what little reference there is to his relationship with the Macedonians is favorable); rather, he is violently criticized for his interference in the affairs of Greek states, and that interference was all too competent and effective. He seems to have understood the Greeks far better than his father, and had far more solid personal connections.

That Antigonus spent much of his time in Athens during this period is further suggested by the fact that his illegitimate son Halkyoneus, whose mother was the Athenian courtesan Demo, was born about 290 BC (Athenaeus 13.578a). Halkyoneus appears as an inexperienced youth fighting alongside his father at Argos in 272 (see below); Antigonus would have been in his late twenties.

During his years as king of Macedonia, Demetrius controlled the city of Athens in two ways: he maintained garrisons at Piraeus and on the Museum Hill in the center of Athens; and he also influenced the selection of magistrates, even though he did not alter the form of government or interfere directly in electoral processes (Plut. *Dem.* 34.4). It may very well be that Antigonus was more welcome in Athens than Demetrius, and the "influence" exerted on the body politic was that of Antigonus. Among the politicians whom Antigonus came to know was Phaidros of Sphettos, whose generalship in

296/5 was mentioned above. He was also elected to several other offices during the next seven years. Phaidros was at the very least cooperative with Demetrius and Antigonus (*I.G.* II², 682). Antigonus was also no doubt acquainted with Olympiodorus, the veteran Athenian politician who was cooperative or at least neutral down to his last appearance in the sources in or about 280 BC. He also held public office in Athens in 294/3 and in 293/2, years in which the influence of Demetrius was high (Paus. 1.26.1; *PHerc.* 1418. col. 30; *I.G.* II², 649, 389). Antigonus was no doubt equally familiar with certain less cooperative politicians. Demochares, a nephew of the great orator Demosthenes, was in self-imposed exile at the court of King Lysimachus of Thrace because of his antipathy to Demetrius (Plut. *Mor.* 851). There was also Kallias of Sphettos, the brother of Phaidros, who spent his entire career in the military service of King Ptolemy of Egypt (The Kallias Decree, published by T. Shear, *Hesperia*, 1978).

Antigonus probably gained additional military, as well as political experience during the nearly seven years that Demetrius was king of Macedonia. Demetrius was an active king, usually outside of Macedonia (which is the reason for much criticism of him as king). There were campaigns against the Aetolians, who later would be on rather friendly terms with Antigonus, and against Pyrrhus. The Pythian Games of 290 were blocked by the Aetolians and Demetrius arranged for them to be held at Athens instead (Plut. *Dem.* 40).

It was probably in the spring of 287 that Demetrius was expelled as king of Macedonia, in circumstances which leave little doubt that the event was carefully planned and coordinated. Macedonia was invaded from the west by King Pyrrhus of Epirus and simultaneously from the east by King Lysimachus of Thrace. A Ptolemaic fleet entered Greek waters and, at about the same time or shortly thereafter, Athens rose in revolt. The impetus for this concerted action against him had been a significant buildup of military might on his part for an announced invasion of Asia, most of it under the control of his rival and now son-in-law Seleucus. Demetrius seemed to be aiming for nothing less than the restoration of Alexander's empire under his leadership. He had warships under construction at Piraeus, Pella, Chalcis, and Corinth; he was collecting mercenaries at Demetrias and other places. Plutarch (*Dem.* 43) gives the totals at this time of 98,000 infantry, 12,000 cavalry, and 500 warships – probably including some "fifteens" and "sixteens".

The event receives only brief and vague reference in several inscriptions and other sources,[12] and so the details must remain unclear. One can speculate that something like the following took place: at the first sign of trouble in Macedonia, Demetrius (who was elsewhere, probably in Demetrias) hastened to Macedonia, and left Antigonus, if he was in Athens at all at the time (he may have been in Corinth or elsewhere) "in charge of Greece" (Plut. *Dem.* 44.2); Antigonus was not present at the final departure of Demetrius from Macedonia. His troops had mutinied; lacking support, he escaped from Macedonia almost alone and began traveling throughout Greece to rebuild his forces. Antigonus was probably not in Athens at the particular time when something happened which resulted in armed activity.

Kallias, an Athenian citizen in mercenary service with Ptolemy, was active with a force of mercenaries in the countryside around Athens, and received some support from a Ptolemaic fleet under the command of Zenon operating nearby. The fleet and Kallias probably arrived in Athens in the early summer of 287 and began planning for a full-scale action against Demetrius. Phaidros, who had been elected hoplite general for 288/7, (*I.G.* II² 682) limited their effectiveness in some way. A line has been excised from the decree in his honor; what remains gives him credit for taking care of the food supply. Kallias and Zenon set up a base on the nearby island of Andros to await events. In July of 287, Phaidros was again elected hoplite general. When the news of the departure of Demetrius from Macedonia reached Zenon and Kallias, probably in the late autumn of 287, they returned to the city. There are five lines excised from the decree for Phaidros at this point. He was apparently deposed from office and a new election was held (the decree refers to Phaidros having been elected general "first;" that is, somebody else was the second person to hold the office in that year). The garrison on the Museum Hill held, and the troops of Demetrius from the Piraeus garrison not only maintained their position but were active against Kallias in the Attic countryside.[13] Kallias achieved some success in bringing in the crops in the following spring. An honorary decree was voted for Zenon in the summer of 286 for this action. At about that time, summer 286 (archon Diocles 286/5), Demochares returned to Athens after receiving large amounts of money from Lysimachus, Ptolemy and even a certain Antipater, probably the surviving son of Cassander, previous king of Macedonia (Plut. *Mor.* 851 d-f). The money was needed for food and mercenaries to enable Athens to withstand the imminent siege by Demetrius. Between his return to Athens and the closing of

17

the city by Demetrius, Demochares made several embassies seeking help and may also have regained Eleusis for Athens, that is, the removal of Demetrius' garrison there (but see below; this may have happened in late 285 or early 284).

Demetrius left Macedonia as a private citizen, abandoned by most of his troops, probably in late summer or early autumn of 287 BC; Antigonus was certainly not with him (he had been left in charge of affairs in Greece), but his wife Phila was. Both escaped to the city of Cassandreia, where Phila ended her life by poison, despondent at the turn of events. Things certainly looked hopeless. Demetrius began making plans to recoup some of his losses. His real goal, after all, had been the conquest of Asia.

The siege of Athens by Demetrius began in the autumn of 286, nearly a year after he left Macedonia; Athens had sought help from Pyrrhus, now joint king of Macedonia, but it was all over before he got there. The money procured by Demochares either was not enough or, for their own reasons, Ptolemy, Pyrrhus, and Lysimachus thought it desirable to negotiate an end to the siege. We do not know with what military strength Demetrius arrived before Athens, but it was enough to encourage negotiations. His travels around Greece for the preceding months must have been successful. Ptolemy sent his diplomatic advisor Sostratos to represent him, Artemidorus of Perinthus represented Lysimachus, Pyrrhus was present in person (as was Demetrius), and the philosopher Crates was chosen to represent the Athenians.[14] There is no certain evidence for the involvement of Antigonus, although it is possible.[15] The terms of the peace were essentially *status quo*. Demetrius accepted his expulsion from Macedonia, but retained his garrisons in Greece, including the Piraeus and the Museum Hill in Athens (Plut. *Dem.* 46.2).

Phaidros seems to have played no further part in the revolt, and there is no certain evidence that Olympiodorus played any part either, although many scholars prefer to see him as the leader of the revolt, and to assume that he also recovered the Museum Hill as a part of this event.[16] It is likely that the leaders of the short-lived revolt were Kallias and Demochares, both of whom had close connections with kings who were actually planning concerted action against Demetrius on all fronts. The activity in Athens was clearly co-ordinated with the invasion of Macedonia by Lysimachus and Pyrrhus and the arrival of the Ptolemaic fleet; Demochares was at the court of Lysimachus, no doubt planning his return to Athens, and Kallias was still in the employ of Ptolemy. The well-laid plans fell apart because of certain unknowns which could not be anticipated: the loyalty of certain Athenians to Demetrius (or at least the unwillingness to oppose him), for example, Phaidros, and probably Olympiodorus as well; the loyalty and competence of his garrisons in Piraeus and Museum Hill; and the resourcefulness of Demetrius himself. The expulsion of Demetrius from Macedonia was accomplished; it was probably too much to expect that he would be completely destroyed. He was weakened, and that was enough for the moment. There was no need for Athens to endure more.

The one certain result of the revolt was that the Athenians took greater control over their internal government; the democracy had continued to exist in form but Demetrius had exerted considerable influence on who held which offices. He would no longer be there to exert that influence, and perhaps there was agreement that Antigonus, who would remain in Greece, would not attempt to influence the Athenians (Plut. *Dem.* 46).

Demetrius sailed off to Asia for his final adventure, while Antigonus, now about thirty-three years old, remained "in charge" of whatever Antigonid possessions remained in Greece. This included Corinth, Demetrias, Chalcis, the Piraeus, the garrison in Athens, and quite a few smaller garrisoned cities, as well as a very uneasy truce with Pyrrhus. When in the summer of 285 Demetrius attacked the possessions of Lysimachus in Asia Minor, Lysimachus induced Pyrrhus to counter by making an invasion of Thessaly, thus threatening one of the strongpoints of Demetrius in Greece, the citadel of Demetrias. Antigonus was successful in turning back Pyrrhus (Plut. *Pyrr.* 12).

Antigonus certainly had his hands full. Demetrius had found much need for military activity in central Greece and the Peloponnese during his reign as king of Macedonia; the problems no doubt remained, exacerbated by the hostility of Pyrrhus and Lysimachus in Macedonia. Antigonus must have had little time to worry about Athens and Attica. A few months later, near the end of winter early in the year 284, Demetrius surrendered to Seleucus. News of the capture of Demetrius precipitated the expulsion of Pyrrhus from his half of Macedonia by Lysimachus, who no longer needed his cooperation. It may also have sparked activity in Athens. The decree honoring Demochares indicates that he recovered Eleusis for Athens not long after his return in the late summer of 286 (Plut. *Mor.* 851 d–f). The decree honoring Philippides lauds his financing of the Eleusinia in the year of Isaios archonship, 284/3 (*I.G.* II^2, 657, lines 39–48). The early summer of 284, after news arrived of the capture of Demetrius, is a likely time for Demochares' recovery of Eleusis, although it could have happened a year earlier, when Antigonus was occupied in Thessaly. The Philippides decree, passed in the year 283/2, contains references to longstanding hopes to someday regain the Piraeus, which clearly has not yet happened (lines 34–35). This same year, 283/2, is the date of a letter of Epicurus which refers to a desire to "destroy the hated Macedonians."[17] Obviously, Athens was restive.

On the news of the capture of Demetrius by Seleucus, Antigonus seems to have done everything humanly possible to secure his father's release (Plut. *Dem.* 51) while continuing to act in his father's name. Only at the death of Demetrius in the autumn of 283 did Antigonus begin to consider himself king, and he did, in fact, later date his kingship from 283 BC.[18] But in 283, he was "king" of very little: he had loyal garrisons in several cities, controlled several ports in Greece, had important "friends" in some cities, and mostly, he had a strong claim to be king of Macedonia. But his was not the only claim, and in fact Lysimachus was currently exercising that power, alone, once he had driven out Pyrrhus. Antigonus Gonatas was only a potential king; the challenge now was to turn potential into reality.

3

ANARCHY AND RECOVERY

The years from 286 to 283 had not been happy ones for Antigonus Gonatas. His father had been deposed as king of Macedonia, his mother had committed suicide, Athens had joined in the hostility against Demetrius, and then the final campaign of Demetrius had proved unsuccessful and fatal. Antigonus had a fleet of some consequence at his disposal; he used it in impressive ceremony to escort the ashes of his father back to Greece for burial in his namesake city of Demetrias (Plut. *Dem.* 53). The Ptolemaic fleet had gained in power and prominence in recent years, at the expense of Demetrius, and no doubt Ptolemy's cooperation was required for the grand display of the Antigonid fleet. This should not be surprising. Over several generations, the relationship between Ptolemies, Seleucids, and Antigonids – and Pyrrhus, also – was one of very aggressive but honorable competition. There was little personal animosity (Lysimachus and Cassander were genuinely hostile to the Antigonids on a personal basis). No doubt there was a sense of the mutability of fortune. Ptolemy I Soter himself would die within a few months; he had already brought his son Philadelphus into full partnership with him, and was aware of the impermanence of worldly power.

Antigonus also had friends and loyal garrison commanders in Greece; some friends would prove to be more constant than others, and not all garrison commanders remained loyal. He must have had some doubts. The garrison at Corinth was by now under the command of his half-brother Craterus (son of Phila and the elder Craterus), whose loyalty was not in doubt. Heracleides commanded the garrison in the Piraeus, and he would prove trustworthy.

The decade between about 285 and 275 BC was clearly a chaotic period; it is more so for us because of the nature of the surviving evidence. We must attempt to piece together events described in isolation in fragmentary sources. Even the relative chronology of events is uncertain; still more controversial are the absolute dates.[19] Nevertheless, it is likely that this decade would seem chaotic even if we had full documentation because it was, in fact, chaotic.

The problem seems to have been too many players on the stage, and almost all of them powerful actors. In a sense, the ultimate cause of the chaos in this decade can be traced to the complex marriage alliances entered into by many of the hellenistic kings, and particularly to the machinations of one woman, Arsinoë II. The events may be briefly described somewhat as follows.

While Demetrius was still alive – although a prisoner of Seleucus – Pyrrhus caused some problems for Antigonus by an invasion of Thessaly and an attempt to dislodge the Antigonid garrisons from some Greek cities. We do not know the details but these efforts met with little success. The real enemy of Pyrrhus was Lysimachus, who successfully drove him out of his half of Macedonia (Plut. *Pyrr.* 12). Lysimachus was also the chief enemy of Antigonus. Not only was he currently ruling the Macedonia to which Antigonus laid claim, but it was Lysimachus, after all, who had offered to pay Seleucus handsomely to kill Demetrius rather than maintain him as a prisoner. Seleucus refused, but news of this attempt certainly did not endear Lysimachus to Antigonus (Plut. *Dem.* 51).

Lysimachus was not much loved by his family either. In 299, Lysimachus had married Arsinoë, daughter of Ptolemy I and Berenice, and at the same time arranged the marriage of his son (by a previous marriage to Nicaea) Agathocles, to Lysandra, the daughter of Ptolemy I and Eurydice. Arsinoë had three sons by Lysimachus, whose position she wished to ensure as against that of her stepson Agathocles and any children by him and her half-sister, Lysandra. When her eldest son, also named Ptolemy, was about seventeen (*c.* 282 BC), she arranged to plant enough suspicion in the mind of Lysimachus so that he executed his son Agathocles. This was an unpopular move in Macedonia, especially with Agathocles' wife Lysandra, who fled for safety and support to Seleucus.

Seleucus attempted to take advantage of this situation and the result was the Battle of Corupedium in early 281, where Lysimachus was defeated in battle and killed. Arsinoë fled to Cassandreia for safety. Shortly thereafter, Seleucus crossed from Asia Minor to Thrace in an attempt to make himself king of Macedonia but was murdered by Ptolemy Ceraunus, a full brother of Lysandra and half-brother to Arsinoë. Ceraunus then proclaimed himself king of

Macedonia. Antigonus, who possessed a significant fleet (because at least a part of Demetrius' fleet had returned to him after the surrender of Demetrius), attempted to invade Macedonia but was repulsed by Ceraunus.[20]

It is in this state of affairs that Pyrrhus decided it would be more useful to respond to the call for help from Tarentum and spend some time conquering Italy and Sicily. He asked for assistance from Ptolemy Ceraunus and from Antigonus Gonatas. He probably received some troops from Ceraunus, although Antigonus apparently did not assist him, in spite of veiled threats from Pyrrhus of the consequences of his refusal (Justin 25.3).

When seen from the vantage point of the Greek cities, which were still nominally independent even though their actions had been somewhat circumscribed by various kings, these years were a perfect opportunity to rearrange things to their liking if possible. It was now that the Achaean League was founded, and this is also approximately when changes of government and the establishment or disestablishment of tyrannies took place in some small cities, and it is probably to this period that one should assign the defection of the mercenary Strombichus and the Athenian capture of the garrison on the Museum Hill in the city of Athens.

An Athenian decree (*I.G.* II² 666, 667) honors Strombichos, who was second in command of the Antigonid garrison on the Museum Hill, because he had decided to betray his commander and assist the Athenians in removing the Macedonian garrison (the event took place at some unspecified earlier time; the decree was passed in 266/5). Pausanias (1.26.3) records a statue of Olympiodorus and summarizes the deeds for which he was honored; the greatest of these was his capture of the Museum garrison, at a time when the Athenians, pondering their former status and the changes of fortune which had befallen them, elected him general. He stormed the fort with old men and boys, and captured the place with very few casualties.

The two events are obviously related. The assistance of the mercenary Strombichos is what made possible the storming of the Museum by Olympiodorus with a small band of old men and boys. The likely time is late in the year 283 or early 282; news of the death of Demetrius had arrived, and this followed full knowledge of the difficulties facing his son Antigonus from Pyrrhus and Lysimachus, the fact that Eleusis had recently been recovered, and that there had been continuous agitation from Lysimachus through the Athenian comic poet Philippides to recover the Piraeus (*I.G.* II² 657, line 35, dated by the archon Euthios to 283/2), and no doubt the Museum as well. Only three years earlier, Athens had acted against Demetrius in connection with his expulsion from Macedonia. That "revolution" was not a complete success (he still garrisoned the Museum and Piraeus), but was not a complete failure either. The lifting of the siege by Demetrius was negotiated almost immediately before any harm was done to Athens, and they had succeeded in removing some Macedonian troops from their midst (the Kallias decree refers to driving the enemy troops out of the city, immediately before mentioning that the Museum was still garrisoned and there was trouble from the Macedonian troops in the Piraeus). More importantly, they had succeeded in regaining almost full control of their internal government: archons were again selected by lot and not appointed by Demetrius (or Antigonus). This string of relative successes and the opportunity provided by the distraction of Antigonus emboldened the Athenians to try to regain the Museum Hill (successfully) and the Piraeus (unsuccessfully).

The reason Olympiodorus could muster only old men and boys was due in part to the fact that many able-bodied men were on mercenary service elsewhere, but mostly to the fact that the best available soldiers were to be used in another, nearly simultaneous operation: the attempt to recover the Piraeus. Polyaenus (5.17.1) records the incident: As with Strombichos at the Museum garrison, the Athenians attempted to subvert an important mercenary, this time Hierocles, a Karian, who was apparently second in command at the Piraeus garrison. He pretended to join their plot, but secretly betrayed them to his commander, Heracleides. When the planned assault took place, the gates were opened by Hierocles to an ambush, and 420 Athenians died in this unsuccessful attempt to regain the Piraeus.[21]

Kallias, the Athenian in mercenary service with Ptolemy, may have been in the city at the time; he was certainly there shortly afterward, no doubt anticipating a reprisal from Antigonus. His decree (Agora I. 7295) records a crisis in the city shortly after the accession of Ptolemy II, early in 282 BC. He used his good relationship with Ptolemy to acquire gifts of money and grain for the city. Perhaps this was a precaution against any impending action by Antigonus in reprisal for the loss of the Museum garrison and the attempt on the Piraeus, but it is just as likely a routine request and grant of the kinds of favor Athens always sought and needed.

There is no record of any subsequent action by Antigonus against Athens. He was, no doubt, fully occupied elsewhere. Apparently other Greek cities, like Athens, took advantage of his seeming weakness and tested his mettle. We have a vague reference in Justin[22] to a war between Antigonus and "the Greek cities" (which ones?) at this time, and another reference to a war between Antigonus and Antiochus of the Seleucid Empire. We know of no significant encounter between Antigonus and Antiochus and, in fact, a peace treaty was eventually signed by these two, which would keep the two dynasties on friendly terms for the next several generations (Justin 25.1).

The "war" of Antigonus with the Greeks seems to have had no major consequences. This is at least partly due to the garrisons that Antigonus controlled at the outset of these troubles. His strongpoint at Demetrias in Thessaly was apparently never seriously threatened, and he maintained garrisons at Chalcis on Euboea as well as in the Attic forts of Rhamnous and Sunium. Of particular value was the strong garrison at Corinth on the isthmus, commanded by his loyal half-brother, Craterus. He maintained control of the Piraeus; the garrison commander was Heracleides, who had been appointed by Demetrius shortly after he left for his Asian expedition late in 286. Heracleides was in command during the unsuccessful Athenian attempt to capture the Piraeus and he was still commanding the garrison at some point between 280 and 277, when he was involved in ransom negotiations for a prisoner under his control, a man named Mithres, who was a former financial official for Lysimachus. The incident almost surely takes place shortly after the death of Lysimachus, who seems not to be involved in the negotiations and would have been if alive. The Athenian Olympiodorus was also involved in these negotiations (*PHerc.* 1418, col. 32), although his precise role is not clear. One might suppose he was acting as an intermediary, something of an "honest broker" between the official negotiators.

Olympiodorus had been supportive of Demetrius earlier, but his successful assault on the Museum Hill was clearly in opposition to Antigonus. A few years later, we again find him in a generally cooperative role during the ransom negotiations for Mithres. One can only surmise that he was first and foremost a patriot, and a practical politician as well. If it were necessary to accept the influence of one of the kings, then Demetrius and later Antigonus were preferable to others, and especially preferable to Cassander and

Lysimachus. But if Antigonus seemed weak, as he must have after the death of Demetrius, and if his future did not look promising, it might be prudent to avoid any support for him, especially if at the same time it also seemed possible to gain real, and not merely nominal, freedom for Athens. The public pressure was certainly there, and it might be better to work with it and perhaps exert some influence on it than to oppose it. The fact that Lysimachus was behind much of the public agitation was no doubt worrisome to him. We simply do not know the details of Athenian politics at this time.

These events can also be viewed through the eyes of the semi-nomadic Gauls to the north of Macedonia. There had been frequent dealings between Macedonians and Gauls over the years, and it had been the function of the Macedonian kings to keep the Gauls out of Macedonia and hence out of Greece. This they did through constant border skirmishes and minor warfare as well as occasionally marrying the daughter of a chief or other diplomatic activity. From the time of Philip II, if not earlier, the less organized Gauls had to deal with a strong Macedonian king. But now there seemed to be some doubt as to who held power in Macedonia. It was a perfect opportunity and it was not lost.

Probably in the summer of 280, three distinct groups of Gauls invaded Macedonia and they would plunder the country regularly for the next several years. Ptolemy Ceraunus was killed in battle, at least partly because he lacked resources after giving some to Pyrrhus for his expedition into Italy. For the next three years there was a succession of kings or power centers in Macedonia, most of whom did not last very long. One, Antipater Etesias, was so-called because he managed to be king for only forty-five days, the period of the etesian winds. Another, Sosthenes, did manage to maintain some control for nearly two years, but refused to take the title of king. There was a Ptolemy, probably the eldest son of Arsinoë and Lysimachus, but he was not maintained in power long either (Justin 24.4–8).

Arsinoe had escaped to Cassandreia after the death of Lysimachus in 281 and she ruled the city for several years. She was persuaded by her half-brother Ptolemy Ceraunus to marry him on the condition that her children would be spared, which she did, and they were not. The eldest, Ptolemy, escaped, but the two younger ones were murdered. With that, Arsinoe left Cassandreia and joined her full brother, Ptolemy Philadelphus, in Alexandria, and she eventually married him. Philadelphus had become king in his own name in 283 on the death of Ptolemy I Soter. Shortly thereafter, Cassandreia came under the control of a tyrant named Apollodorus, probably with the help of a Spartan exile named Cleonymus.[23]

Meanwhile, Antigonus was not idle. No doubt the troubled conditions in Greece demanded much of his attention, but he eventually found the opportunity to engage a large force of Gauls near Lysimacheia, probably in the summer of 277. Although the details are confused, he managed to lure them into a trap with the promise of plunder. He displayed all manner of royal munificence to them, including an impressive fleet of warships and a large contingent of elephants, implying that they might possess some or all of this. With more attention to profit than caution, the Gauls fell into an ambush. A large force of Gauls was virtually annihilated and Antigonus was seen as something of a hero throughout Greece. The philosopher Menedemos of Eretria made the motion for the decree to honor Antigonus as savior of the Greeks (D.L. 2.136).

Although Antigonus was the sole victor in this battle, Athenian ships also saw service against the Gauls.[24] This was a common Greek undertaking and clearly Antigonus and Athens (and no doubt others) were working for the same goal. Athens, of course, still had a navy, and it could be based nowhere but at the Piraeus, which was under the control of Antigonus. It is probably to this time that a decree (*I.G.* II^2, 677) in honor of Heracleitus should be dated. The stone is broken at the top, so no archon name survives. Heracleitus is honored for his actions "against the barbarians on behalf of Greek safety" (line 6) and for his "friendship and benefaction toward King Antigonus and the *boule* and *demos* of Athens." Heracleitus, son of Asclepiades, was an Athenian citizen of the deme Athmonon, who maintained a long association with Antigonus and ultimately was appointed garrison commander at the Piraeus.[25]

Antigonus was now in a position to make gains in Macedonia. He brought the city of Cassandreia under siege, and took it by yet another trick, this time with the help of an archpirate named Ameinias.[26] Ameinias was to pretend to betray Antigonus, enter the city and once in, open the gates to Antigonus (the same ruse, hardly original, had been used on Antigonus by the Athenians twice – once successfully). It is worth noting that the activity of Antigonus in Macedonia at this time was conducted largely with mercenaries, including Gallic mercenaries against other Gauls, and with people called "pirates." His more seasoned mercenaries and veteran troops were no doubt on duty in the Greek garrisons.

Antigonus had never recognized the expulsion of Demetrius from Macedonia, and had called himself "King of Macedonia" since the death of Demetrius in 283. Now, in 276, he seemed secure in the actual control of Macedonia. Lysimachus was dead and his kingdom dismembered. The Gauls had been beaten back. An understanding had been reached with the house of Seleucus and there would be no challenge from that quarter. That understanding may have included the arrangements for the marriage of Antigonus to his niece, Phila, daughter of his sister Stratonike and Seleucus. The wedding probably took place in 276 or 275, to judge by the age at later times of their son Demetrius II. It was about time: Antigonus was already well over forty years of age (his bride was probably about eighteen).[27] It might be a good time to reflect on the proper means of governing Macedonia. There was, however, no time for that. There was at least one more threat: Pyrrhus was about to return from Italy.

4

THE STRUGGLE WITH
PYRRHUS

Pyrrhus returned from Italy in 274 BC with a grudge to settle against Antigonus, who had refused to send help to Pyrrhus while he was in Italy and Sicily, and whose pleasure at the removal of Pyrrhus from Macedonia was probably not well concealed. Pyrrhus was also in the mood for success; after all, his adventure in Italy had ultimately been unsuccessful. He still controlled Epirus; that was not in doubt. He could not raise very many forces from that source alone, however, and added a large contingent of Gallic mercenaries to his invasion force of Macedonia.

This was to be a mere plundering expedition, according to Plutarch (*Pyrr.* 26.3–4), but events turned out otherwise and Pyrrhus could always take advantage of opportunities. Antigonus was defeated in battle at least once, and perhaps more than once. He tacitly conceded control of western and central Macedonia to Pyrrhus and occupied only the coastal area. Pyrrhus would soon abandon his gains in Macedonia for new adventures in the Peloponnese, but his success in Macedonia is an indication of his personal popularity and reputation as well as the fact that Antigonus had not been able to solidify his control of Macedonia. There were many defections from his troops, largely Gallic mercenaries, and perhaps much of the population of Macedonia was of uncertain loyalty.

To be a Macedonian citizen, residing in Macedonia in the early third century BC, must have been a very difficult thing indeed. The older men remembered the time when Cassander was king and, although he may not have been the best or the most popular king in Macedonian history, at least one knew who the king was and expected him to remain in that position with no serious challenges. Even the reign of Demetrius must have looked like a time of stability compared to what followed. Demetrius was guilty only of neglect of citizens; at least Macedonia did not suffer invasions under his rule. The subsequent division of the kingdom between Lysimachus and Pyrrhus would take some time to get used to, but there was no time. Pyrrhus was soon expelled, and there was no time for Lysimachus to seem a normal and natural part of the landscape before he, too, was no longer in the picture. And then came a succession of kings, invasion by Gauls, and general anarchy. The Macedonians now had another king, Antigonus the son of Demetrius, but how long would he last? It had been ten years since anyone could feel certain about anything.

So, when Pyrrhus invaded Macedonia, he had friends from his previous occupation of the country, and a very good track record. He was at least as well known in Macedonia as Antigonus, and in spite of all his other adventures he had managed consistently to be king of Epirus for several decades, a record Antigonus Gonatas did not have.

Even in relatively absolutist monarchies, popular sentiment still plays an important role. Pyrrhus made a serious mistake in allowing his Gallic mercenaries to plunder the royal tombs at Aegae and go unpunished.[28] It is true that Antigonus never conceded anything: he was still king of Macedonia and Pyrrhus was a temporary interloper. It is probably also true that Antigonus did his best to stir up resentment against Pyrrhus. He, too, had many friends and connections in Macedonia. In any case, after the destruction and looting of royal tombs, Pyrrhus became very unpopular and his control of part of Macedonia was tenuous at best. At that point, he received a request from Cleonymus, an exiled Spartan king, to lead an army against Sparta in the interest of Cleonymus. A new adventure was very appealing under the circumstances, and it was probably much more than an adventure. It is clear enough that Antigonus had considerable strength in the Peloponnese. Indeed, the announced reason for the expedition of Pyrrhus to the Peloponnese, to "set free the cities which were subject to Antigonus" must have had some basis in fact even if exaggerated (Plut. *Pyrr.* 26.10).

Pyrrhus led a large invasion force of 25,000 infantry and 2,000 cavalry against Sparta, which was weakly defended.[29] King Areus was in Crete with a large part of the Spartan military force, and Pyrrhus was no doubt aware of that. Antigonus was aware of it too, and took steps to save the situation. With the help of the women, Sparta held out against Pyrrhus for one night, and on the following day a relieving force arrived from Corinth commanded by Antigonus' old friend, the archpirate Ameinias. On the following day, King Areus returned from Crete and Pyrrhus was forced to withdraw. His retreat was subject to strong harassment by King Areus, during which Pyrrhus' son, Ptolemy, was killed. This Ptolemy had been left in charge of Epirus while Pyrrhus was in Italy, even though he was only about fifteen years old, and was the heir-apparent of Pyrrhus.

Pyrrhus then withdrew to Argos, where he had been summoned to aid one of two warring factions in the city. The other faction had invited Antigonus to come to the city. He arrived before Pyrrhus and seized the high ground. The resulting battle at Argos was characterized by all the bad things common to warfare: miscommunication, plans not well made going awry, darkness, confusion, and treachery. Pyrrhus had managed to lead part of his forces into the city at night, but not well. A night of confusion and panic was followed by hand to hand fighting in the narrow city streets at daybreak. While Pyrrhus was trying, unsuccessfully, to withdraw from the city, he was killed by a blow to the head from a roof tile thrown by an old woman who thought her soldier son was in danger from Pyrrhus. The blow may not have been fatal, but the severing of his head by one of Antigonus' soldiers was. Halkyoneus, the illegitimate son of Antigonus, presented the head to his father, who was not at all happy to receive it. Antigonus struck his son and called him a barbarian; he was reportedly moved to tears, and reflected on the mutability of fortune. The remains of Pyrrhus were given to his son Helenus for burial and Halkyoneus was later praised by Antigonus for his humane treatment of Helenus and other supporters of Pyrrhus. Pyrrhus received a royal burial, and his surviving son Helenus was sent back to Epirus, where he reigned without interference from Antigonus.

Antigonus had considered Pyrrhus a worthy adversary, a man of his own rank and status whose military ability earned him grudging respect. He likened Pyrrhus to a good dice player who makes many good throws but doesn't know what to do with them (Plut. *Pyrr.* 26.2). On another occasion, when asked who in his opinion was the greatest general, he said "Pyrrhus, if he lives to be old" (*Pyrr.* 8.2). Pyrrhus was not yet fifty years old when he died.

With the death of Pyrrhus in 272 Antigonus was secure as King of Macedonia. But he was potentially much more than that. Indeed, he had already built a considerable power base in Greece, which had sustained him and made him a force to be reckoned with even when he had no power in Macedonia. Macedonian kings had existed prior to Philip II, but they did not matter very much. Some kind of domination or control of Greece was necessary.

5

THE GREEK HEGEMONY

Even if he had wanted to, Antigonus could not turn back the clock and rule a small Macedonian kingdom that was self sufficient and somewhat isolated from the rest of the world. Indeed, even in those apparently simpler days, Macedonia was always subject to the interference of outside powers – Persia or Athens or other Greek adventurers – not to mention incursions of barbarians from the north. With most of the civilized world ruled by large empires founded by Macedonians and deeply imbued with Greek culture, Macedonia and Greece must either be on an equal footing with the other empires or absorbed by one of them.

Antigonus inherited a system of garrisons and personal connections in Greece from Demetrius. His bitter experience in the decade of chaos after the death of Demetrius taught him to refine and modify that system. The end result was a rather coherent system of maintaining a Greek hegemony with minimum use of resources. The Antigonid presence in Greece was constant and pervasive; no one living in Greece had to travel very far to find someone who reported to Antigonus. A glance at the map reveals that Antigonus had at least the potential to control entry and exit into the Greek mainland. For all, or most, of his long forty-year reign, garrisons were in place at Corinth, Troezen, Epidaurus, Megara, Salamis, Eleusis, Piraeus, Sunium, Rhamnous, Chalcis, and Eretria. These connected very well with his major capital at Demetrias in Thessaly, a large fortified city totally under his control which could easily house 20,000 to 25,000 troops. In addition, Antigonus maintained important political connections with local politicians in all of these cities as well as with Athens, Argos, Megalopolis, Elis, the Aetolian League, and to some degree the Achaean League as well.

Corinth was garrisoned in 303 BC by Demetrius Poliorcetes, at

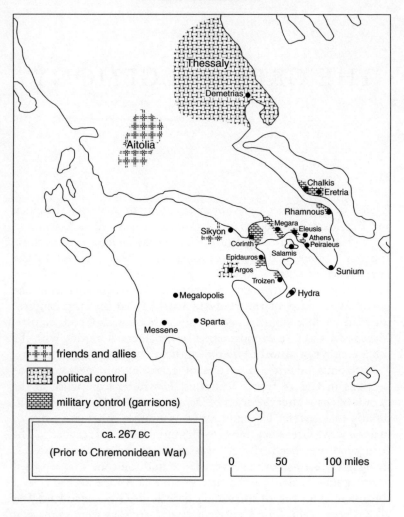

friends and allies

political control

military control (garrisons)

ca. 267 BC

(Prior to Chremonidean War)

0   50   100 miles

which time he also attempted to revive the Hellenic League established by Philip II in 338 (D.S. 20.103). The league functioned only briefly under Demetrius, and there is no indication that Antigonus ever sought to revive it. In fact, it probably suited his purposes better that the league not exist. For a long time, the garrison at Corinth was commanded by Craterus, the half-brother of Antigonus. Because of his personal connection with Demetrius and Antigonus, his role was much greater than that of a mere commander of troops. It was his responsibility to act as liaison between Antigonus and the political groups and individuals within the city of Corinth.[30] Not much is known about the government of Corinth, but here as elsewhere the practice of Antigonus seems to have been to allow the maximum degree of internal autonomy, with forms of government unchanged from tradition, so long as the individuals exercising political power were friendly – or at least not hostile – to Antigonus. Also based at Corinth for many years was the archpirate Ameinias, who is known to have led a force to Sparta in 272 from Corinth (Plut. *Pyrr.* 29.6). Since the date of death of Craterus is unknown, it is even possible that Ameinias was in a significant position of command at Corinth after the death of Craterus. Craterus is last mentioned in the sources when he led an unsuccessful rescue force to Elis *c.* 271 to support a tyrant who was a friend of Antigonus.[31] Craterus' son Alexander also held the position as commander at Corinth *c.* 252 BC, when he revolted from Antigonus and declared himself an independent king. Alexander was joined in his rebellion by the garrisons at Chalcis and Eretria, which has led some scholars to suggest that Alexander was in fact in charge of all three garrisons.[32] It is much more likely that he simply had partners in crime, that here was a conspiracy of three garrison commanders to rebel from Antigonus. Alexander was simply the most powerful of the three. It is worth noting that none of the garrison commanders seemed to have any specific title or clearly defined duties. Their influence and their duties depended entirely upon their relationship with Antigonus and other personal connections. Craterus, for example, was the half-brother of the king and the relationship between the two was personally very close. This was known to all (Plut. *Mor.* 219b); Craterus was almost a joint king with Antigonus and his authority went far beyond commanding troops at Corinth. He seems to have had full authority to arrange ransom of prisoners (*PHerc.* 1418, discussed earlier in Chapter 2), and busied himself with making a collection of Athenian decrees. His son Alexander, on the other hand, no doubt had his position because he was a blood relative of the king, but the personal affection was lacking. Ameinias, the former pirate who held some significant position at Corinth, almost made up for his lack of status by his close personal relationship with Antigonus. Alexander, son of Craterus, died about five years later and Antigonus recovered control of Corinth by promising the widow, Nicaea, a marriage to his son Demetrius. She consented and handed over the garrison, but the marriage did not take place.[33] No more is heard of her. For the next few years, there seem to be three simultaneous commanders at Corinth. This is misleading. The philosopher Persaios, a man named Archelaus, and another named Theophrastus are all referred to in terms that suggest they are in charge of something. What is most likely is that Persaios was the major commander, the one with most influence with Antigonus and the best political connections within the city. Archelaus and Theophrastus were generally subordinate to him and had functions that were more military than civil.[34]

Antigonus lost Corinth to Aratus of Sicyon in 243 BC and it was not recovered during his lifetime. The garrison was taken by force and the city joined the Achaean League, headed by Aratus, who had procured some inside help from disaffected mercenaries within the garrison. It is not surprising that most of the troops in the garrison were mercenaries of diverse origin, and the turnover of personnel was probably great. Aratus had befriended four brothers who are called "Syrian;" with generous gifts of cash he procured the necessary information from them. One can wonder about the source of the money: Aratus had made several trips to Ptolemy in Egypt and Ptolemy had long been a good source of funds for anyone opposed to Antigonus. Aratus hired 400 mercenaries and with a sudden night attack overwhelmed the garrison, which resisted strenuously with great loss of life (Plut. *Arat.* 24). Even Polybius, a source generally hostile to Antigonus, did not approve of a sneak attack in peacetime and considered the event shameful (Polyb. 2.50.9). The news was no doubt very disconcerting to Antigonus, if for no other reason than that he had lost something which he had held for so long. As a practical matter, however, it seems not to have affected his position in Greece because of the strength of the rest of the system.

The city of Troezen not far from Corinth would have been a likely place for the installation of an Antigonid garrison. There is in fact evidence for a garrison at some few points in time. In or about 275 BC, a garrison of Antigonus commanded by a man named Eudamidas was attacked and expelled by the Spartan exile Cleonymus (Polyaen.

2.29.1). There is an inscription which suggests a garrison at some other date, which is probably at a later period of time.[35] One cannot be certain if the garrison expelled by Cleonymus was reinstalled, but when one looks at the entire plan and situation of Antigonus in Greece, it would have been a high priority. Indeed, during the Chremonidean War, Troezen is not among the list of those allied with Athens. Troezen and Athens had for long been allies and friends and one must wonder why Troezen did not join her traditional ally in the struggle against Antigonus; it may be because it was impossible due to the presence of an Antigonid garrison. In 243 BC, shortly after the capture of Corinth by Aratus, Troezen was one of three cities which were brought into the Achaean League by Aratus of Sicyon (Plut. *Arat.* 24.3; Paus. 2.8.5; Polyb. 2.43.4).

Epidaurus is another of those cities brought into the Achaean League at that time. There is no other firm evidence for a garrison at Epidaurus; however, the location is appropriate if Antigonus had planned to control entry into the nearby Saronic Gulf. During the Chremonidean War, the Ptolemaic fleet under Patroclus was not able to accomplish anything in the western end of the gulf, and was forced to utilize a base camp near Sunium in Attica. Antigonus may have maintained garrisons not only at Troezen and Epidaurus, but also on the island of Hydra which guards the entrance to the gulf. The only possible evidence for this is an anecdote in Plutarch's life of Aratus (Plut. *Arat.* 12) indicating that Aratus was blown off course on the way to Egypt and landed at an island called "Adria" which had an Antigonid garrison. The text is apparently corrupt, and Hydra is one of the possibilities. It is the possibility which makes the best strategic sense.

Megara is the other of the three cities that joined the Achaean League in 243, and it seems to have held an Antigonid garrison for most of the earlier time. It was held by Demetrius (*Syll.*[3] 331 and Plut. *Dem.* 39), and contained an Antigonid garrison, mostly Gauls, during the Chremonidean War (Polyaen. 4.6.3; Trogus, *Prol.* 26) and at some uncertain date around the middle of the third century Megara contained a garrison commanded by a man named Lycinus, an exile from one of the Greek cities of south Italy (Stobaeus, *Peri Xenes* 40.8).

One of the two strongest garrisons ringing the Saronic Gulf (the other was Corinth) was the Antigonid garrison at the Piraeus. A strong garrison was established by Demetrius in 295 after the expulsion of the tyrant Lachares, and Antigonid control of the

Piraeus was probably continuous from that point until its loss to Athens in 229 BC during the reign of Antigonus Doson. There is evidence for the existence of the garrison datable to 286, 277, 265, 252, and 239. We may have an almost complete list of garrison commanders (the commander(s) for the first ten years, prior to Heracleides in 286, are not known): Heracleides, Hierocles, Heracleitus, and Diogenes.[36]

The interaction between at least some members of the garrison and local citizens was sometimes rather close, and was probably expected to be. The first two garrison commanders were mercenaries and foreigners. Heracleides seems to have been not well liked, and not much is known about him. Hierocles, who commanded the garrison sometime before 265, was a close personal friend of the philosopher Menedemos and was stationed at the garrison for many years as a subordinate to Heracleides before becoming commander in his own name. It was in that earlier time that the Athenians thought they knew him well enough to bribe him to betray the garrison to a group of Athenians. He pretended to go along with it, but informed his superior of the plot and an ambush was set. The third commander of the Piraeus garrison was an Athenian citizen by the name of Heracleitus; he is known to have been in command c. 252 BC, at the time of the revolt of Alexander, son of Craterus, at Corinth. The association of the Athenian Heracleitus with Antigonus went back many years; he was honored by the Athenians for his involvement in the battle of Lysimacheia, at which Antigonus defeated a large group of Gauls. (*I.G.* II², 677).

The Piraeus garrison was commanded by one Diogenes in 239 BC (Plut. *Arat.* 34.1) but it is not certain how long he had been in that position, or whether he had been appointed by Antigonus or his son and successor Demetrius II. He commanded the garrison for 10 years, until in 229 he was induced to turn the garrison over to the Athenians, for which he was rewarded with Athenian citizenship.

For the other forts in Attica (Eleusis, Salamis, Sunium, Rhamnous, among others) we have no certain evidence of continuous Antigonid garrisons. To the extent that the forts were under Athenian control, the local commander may nevertheless have had to work closely with the commander of the Piraeus; their local autonomy was ambiguous at best. Some of the outlying forts, if under control of an Antigonid garrison, may have reported to the commander of the Piraeus. We do have evidence for garrison commanders at these forts; there are some honorary decrees reporting that an individual was "appointed by the king." But that designation seems to apply to those years just after the Chremonidean War when Antigonus appointed most Athenian officials. Some of the garrison commanders are both appointed by the king and elected by the people, as though the one process is a ratification of the other.[37] Strategic considerations rather than solid evidence compel one to suppose that most of the garrisons were held by Antigonus, or controlled by him in some way, throughout most of his reign. Events took the turn they did during the Chremonidean War because the garrisons were controlled by Antigonus at that time; his control and influence in Attica was even greater in the period after the Chremonidean War.

The Antigonid garrisons at Chalcis and Eretria are largely assumed. Demetrius had ships prepared for his invasion of Asia in 287 in the harbor at Chalcis (Plut. *Dem.* 43). One assumes that if he were building warships and maintaining them in the harbor that he exerted some influence or control in the city. There was probably a garrison in Chalcis, and there is no known time before 252 when it would have been lost. If it was, it was not for long, because by the time of the Chremonidean War the region was quite secure. A garrison at Chalcis would explain that security. Chalcis rebelled against Antigonus along with Alexander the son of Craterus in 252. It was presumably recovered along with Corinth in 247, because it contained a Macedonian garrison later, until the time when the Roman Flamininus ordered the evacuation of the garrisons in 196 BC.

Similar assumptions must be made about Eretria. It was strategically less essential, but there is some evidence for a garrison at an early date. The philosopher Menedemos, a citizen of Eretria, was a close friend of Antigonus. The brief biography of Menedemos by Diogenes Laertius relates the exile of Menedemos because of his close friendship with Antigonus, and that Menedemos was unhappy at the capture of Eretria, and his request to Antigonus to grant the city freedom. All of this must take place sometime prior to the death of Menedemos *c.* 265 BC (Diogenes Laertius 2.127 and 2.142). Although these references are confusing, it is clear that Antigonus exerted some sort of influence and very likely had a garrison in the city of Eretria prior to 265. There was no opportunity to lose the garrison until *c.* 252, when that garrison may have rebelled along with Alexander the son of Craterus at Corinth. If it was lost then, it was later recovered; there is an Antigonid garrison recorded in an inscription dated to 236 BC (*SEG* XXV.155) honoring the commander Dicaiarchus.

These garrisons were strategically placed. The garrison at Corinth isolated all states in the Peloponnesus from the remainder of Greece. The garrisons at Megara and at Chalcis isolated Attica from central Greece. It was thus difficult for Greek states to combine militarily against Antigonus. There was little direct control of states in the Peloponnesus, but this was not necessary in as much as any action originating in the Peloponnesus could be blocked at Corinth. The garrisons also served to control major naval landing places in southern Greece. The occupation of Corinth made possible some control of naval activity in both the Corinthian and the Saronic Gulfs. The garrison at the Piraeus occupied another important commercial harbor and added to the control of the Saronic Gulf. The garrisons at Sunium and Troezen could watch the entrance to the Saronic Gulf. Sunium, Rhamnous and Chalcis guarded the approach and passage of the Eurippus channel between Euboea and the Greek mainland.

The strongest garrison of all, of course, was Demetrias in Thessaly, the fortress city founded by Demetrius Poliorcetes in 294 (Plut. *Dem.* 53.4; Strabo 9.5.15). This large and well-fortified city provided secure communication between southern Greece and Macedonia proper.[38] It was the door to Macedonia, while the other garrisons in Greece were the outer fences.

Garrisons alone might not be enough to secure the interests of Antigonus in Greece, and in some cases, they were not even necessary. The connections of Antigonus with philosophical schools in Athens and with other Athenians have already been noted. Even the Chremonidean War (see chapter 6) was only a brief hiatus in the otherwise friendly relations of Antigonus with Athens. After the successful conclusion of the war, he found it prudent to install a garrison on the Museum Hill and to take over the operation of the city government to the extent of naming the major officials (Apollodoros *FGrH* 244 F44; Paus. 3.6.6). But that only lasted for about five years. He removed the garrison from the Museum Hill *c.* 255 BC because it was no longer necessary. Athens would conduct itself in ways corresponding to his interests without the presence of an expensive garrison. This is perhaps best demonstrated by the fact that when Alexander, son of Craterus, rebelled with his garrison at Corinth and took Chalcis and Eretria with him, Athens was invited to join and refused to do so. Indeed, Alexander apparently attempted to apply force to bring Athens to his side, and with the aid of Aristomachus of Argos, another friend of Antigonus, Athens resisted any attempt to join Alexander in his rebellion against Antigonus

(*I.G.* II², 774, a decree honoring Aristomachus). Athens also refused to join Aratus of Sicyon in his opposition to Antigonus in the years after 243 BC (Plut. *Arat.* 24). There are several inscriptions indicating that Athens rather regularly would make public sacrifices for the welfare of the King of Macedonia and his queen. Athens remained loyal to Antigonus, and so preserved its internal autonomy.³⁹

Argos maintained close and friendly relations with Antigonus throughout his long reign and for some time afterwards. At some time well before 272 BC, Aristippus had made himself tyrant in Argos. He was challenged in 272 by Aristeas who sought the aid of Pyrrhus. This event brought Pyrrhus to the Peloponnesus and brought Antigonus directly to Argos to aid his friend Aristippus, resulting in the death of Pyrrhus (Plut. *Pyrr.* 30). We hear no more of Aristippus, but he was succeeded by his son Aristomachus who was in power in Argos by 255 BC (*I.G.* II², 774). He was killed by his slaves in 242, but immediately followed as tyrant by his son Aristippus, who was in turn killed in battle but succeeded by another relative, probably a brother, named Aristomachus. He maintained the family tyranny until after 229 BC (Plut. *Arat.* 25–29). This was a useful connection for Antigonus. Except for the rescue mission in 272, it required no deployment of troops, yet resulted in control of the Argolid and a reliable check to any other hostile activity in the Peloponnesus. Argos was a traditional enemy of Sparta, and Sparta was probably the only possible source of hostility in the Peloponnesus. There is no record of any overt activity on the part of Aristomachus of Argos during the Chremonidean War; however, the existence of a friendly Argos at that particular geographic location complicated the plans of the Ptolemaic fleet and also made the land march of King Areus of Sparta a little more difficult. He could count on no help along the way and some possible harassment. Antigonus did not seem to need much more than this in that episode. When help was needed it was forthcoming. When Alexander son of Craterus rebelled from his position at Corinth, Aristomachus of Argos took action against him (*I.G.* II², 774); the details are not preserved on the broken stone but it is clear that there was some military engagement and that Aristomachus went so far as to furnish Athens with money from his own resources to enable Athens to preserve its independence. Argos was important enough for Antigonus to ensure his personal involvement when necessary. In addition to the rescue mission in 272, Antigonus seems to have been involved in a series of assassination attempts against Aratus of Sicyon – this in return for attempts by Aratus on the life of Aristippus. (Plut. *Arat.* 26.1).

The assumption that Antigonus had friendly relations with the city of Megalopolis is largely inferential. The fact that Megalopolis was ruled by a tyrant for much of the third century does not necessarily connect the city with Antigonus in any way. There is no firm evidence that Antigonus supported tyrants as a matter of preference; rather, he supported governments that were friendly to him, whatever their form. This particular tyranny was constantly at odds with Sparta and was invaded by Sparta on several occasions. Sparta was traditionally hostile to Antigonus. It is a weak argument to assume that the enemy of one's enemy must be a friend, but one can add to this the fact that the historian Polybius was a citizen of Megalopolis, whose family was of the opposing political faction to the tyranny of Aristodemus. Polybius is perhaps the source most hostile to Antigonus, and the source for the allegation that Antigonus supported tyrants (Polyb. 10.22). Megalopolis was in any case not worse than neutral toward Antigonus; there is no record of any difficulties whatsoever between Antigonus or any of his friendly allies, and Megalopolis.

There is only a brief mention in our sources of the situation at Elis, and it would seem that Antigonus had an ally in that city in the person of a tyrant named Aristotimus. At some time shortly after 272, Aristotimus was faced with an uprising and Craterus rushed to his aid from Corinth. He arrived too late, however, and Aristotimus was dead when he arrived. The tyranny was ended; Craterus took no action to reinstall a tyranny but merely left, apparently on friendly terms with the inhabitants (Justin 26.1; Paus. 5.5.1; Plut. *Mor.* 251A and 253A). This seems to be an example of a situation where Antigonus took an opportunity to extend his influence. It was not part of a master plan; Elis was not essential to his purposes. But it would be desirable to have a friend in power in Elis if that were conveniently arranged. So long as the Isthmus, the eastern Peloponnesus, and Attica were secure, the western Peloponnesus was a desirable addition but not essential.

Antigonus made use of tyrants, like garrisons, when it seemed necessary, appropriate, and possible. Geography and population were more important to him than form of government. Specific information is available for only very few cities, primarily those ruled by tyrants, because the tyrannies later became very unpopular and later writers had something to say about them. There may well have been many other cities in which Antigonus exercised considerable influence, which caused no notice to be made in later sources.

Antigonus was able to work with a confederation of autonomous cities quite as easily as with tyrants, if it suited his interests. The best example of this is the Aetolian League. Throughout the long reign of Antigonus, there is no record of any hostility on the part of Aetolia, and there were certainly opportunities. The friendship between Antigonus and the Aetolians went back at least to 280 BC, when the Aetolians are referred to by Justin (24.1) as allies of Antigonus in the struggle with Ptolemy Ceraunus. There was no open alliance between the two, nothing that would have required Aetolia to offer aid to Antigonus against Pyrrhus, for example. But there does seem to have been a tacit agreement not to get in each other's way. During the Chremonidean War, the Aetolian League was explicitly neutral, and sought to secure the safety of religious meeting places.[40] This neutrality is of considerable importance. Had the Aetolians joined the opposition to Antigonus in the Chremonidean War, the strategic situation, the resources on each side, and the outcome very likely would be much different. Polybius makes several references to a formal agreement between the Aetolians and Antigonus to partition the territory of the Achaean League, although nothing seems to have come of it.[41] If true, it would be the first formal agreement between the two but it is noteworthy that the long relationship between the two powers made such a treaty at least believable. The inference of good diplomatic relationships with the Aetolian League is finally confirmed by the placement of Antigonid garrisons in Greece. They were not designed to ward off any threat from the direction of Aetolia.

The relationship of Antigonus with the newer Achaean League was less successful. Polybius[42] recounts that many of the cities which eventually became the Achaean League had been garrisoned by Antigonus and had tyrants imposed on them by him. No details are available, and so we cannot know if garrisons and tyrants were short-term or longer, in which cities, and if a friendly relationship was developed with the removal of tyrants. In at least one city, Sicyon, we know that Antigonus carefully cultivated friendship with Cleinias, an important politician in Sicyon, and later with his son Aratus, who would become the most influential official of the Achaean League (Plut. *Arat.* 2, 4, 13, *passim*). Aratus ultimately became quite hostile to Antigonus and the situation never improved. Plutarch's statement that Antigonus was "jealous" because Sicyon had "regained its freedom" under Aratus (Plut. *Arat.* 9.3) probably merely refers to Antigonus' frustration at being unable to influence Aratus, and suggests that Antigonus had previously enjoyed amicable relations with the city. There was a royal horse farm near the city (Plut. *Arat.* 6), which implies at least moderately friendly relations; it would have been foolish to have such an installation in unfriendly territory. The horse farm may not have outlasted the enmity of Aratus.

Over the years, Antigonus had established considerable control and influence in Greece, based on a strategically located show of force and opportunistic ties of friendship and alliance. His network of friends and agents had two objectives. One was to make it difficult for any non-Greek power (Ptolemy or, less likely, Seleucus) to intervene in Greek affairs without automatically encountering resistance and without his knowledge. Also, any combination of forces within Greece directed against him would be unable to do so in secrecy and would encounter logistical difficulties in maintaining communication and effecting movement. The Chremonidean War was the test of the system, and the system worked.

6

THE
CHREMONIDEAN
WAR

The system of garrisons and allies established by Antigonus left plenty of room for local maneuvering. The Greek cities and leagues, by themselves, could not directly threaten his position in Macedonia or his position as a "great power" in the hellenistic world after Alexander, but they could cause him nearly constant annoyance and require his frequent attention. That was the price he paid for being king, the price he especially had to pay for exercising a hegemony over Greece on the cheap. The loose system required very little in the way of manpower and did not require him to actually administer Greek cities. This meant that someone else (local politicians) would manage things. If their actions were inimical to his interests, he was in a position to intervene, but he took no overt action until or unless necessary.

The only real threat to Antigonus was Ptolemy Philadelphus of Egypt. His power was at least as great, greater depending on how one measured it. Ptolemy was certainly wealthier and may have had a larger fleet, but he did not have a land army equal to Antigonus. The chief threat resided in the fact that Ptolemy was a Macedonian, albeit one who ruled Egypt. He wanted and needed a connection with "home" – Macedonia and Greece – for sentimental as well as practical reasons. No man is an island, not even Ptolemy with all his wealth; he needed a large cadre of Greek/Macedonian ruling officials, as well as mercenaries, to assist him in Egypt, and they could be maintained only with some of the comforts of home, some sense of familiarity. This is at least a large part of the reason behind the development of the Museum and related institutions in Alexandria. To maintain some influence and interest in Greek affairs was also a necessity. It also suited his interests to keep Antigonus as weak and uninfluential as possible. No one had quite forgotten that Antigonus

was the son of the Demetrius who, twenty years earlier, had tried
and almost succeeded in conquering all of Asia, and that he was the
grandson of the Antigonus who, a little over thirty years earlier, had
almost conquered all of Alexander's empire.

Hostility between the Ptolemies of Egypt and the Antigonids of
Macedonia was long-standing and remained a feature of Hellenistic
geopolitics. Hostility between the Ptolemies and the Seleucids of
Asia was not much less, and indeed, the so-called "Second Syrian
War" between these two is nearly contemporaneous with the
Chremonidean War. The Antigonids and Seleucids maintained
friendly or at least neutral relations, especially in the preceding two
decades, but there is no evidence for a formal alliance in either the
Chremonidean War or the Second Syrian War, nor for any direct
involvement of one in support of the other.

Ptolemy controlled parts of Syria and Asia Minor, in contention
with the Seleucids. He also exercised some control or hegemony over
many of the Aegean islands, in contention with Antigonus, who does
not seem to have placed a high priority on any hegemony or influence
in the islands, beyond whatever opportunity offered. Ptolemy
attempted to exert influence on the cities of mainland Greece,
without much success prior to the Chremonidean War because
most of the Greek cities were under a rather tight hegemony of
Antigonus Gonatas.

So, it was due to continuous Ptolemaic agitation that in the spring
of 264 BC (the archonship of Peithidemos, Athenian archon year
265/4)[43] an alliance was formed between Ptolemy, Athens, Sparta,
the Elians, Achaeans, Tegeans, Mantineans, Orchomenians (Arca-
dian), Phialians, Kaphueans, and "some" Cretans (I.G. II², 687)
against Antigonus Gonatas. The decree recording the alliance and
declaration of war was moved by the Athenian Chremonides, (who
spent most of his adult life as a mercenary in the service of Ptolemy)
hence the name of the war. The list of allies is revealing. Many were
Spartan dependencies, all were militarily insignificant, none strategically located (except perhaps Athens, if she had controlled her port
and border forts, which she did not). More important is the long list
of Greek entities which were not among the allies (such as Corinth,
Argos, Troezen, Megara, Thebes, Megalopolis, and Sicyon), either
because they were garrisoned by Antigonus or because they were not
sufficiently hostile to him.

The declaration of war offers no specific grievances by any party,
but merely states in very general terms that Antigonus is unjust and

a breaker of treaties. One can wonder which treaty, with whom, and what conditions were violated, but in fact we have no record of any treaty between Antigonus and any of the parties to this war. There are references to ongoing hostilities during the previous two years, in the archonships of Menekles and Nikias.[44] Nor can we overlook the possible influence of personal relationships: of course, Ptolemy and Antigonus were well acquainted and were in fact related by marriage, but Chremonides may have been well acquainted with Antigonus as well in that both had been long-time students of Zeno, although probably not at the same time.[45] Unfortunately, and perhaps curiously, we have no information of any action by Chremonides during the ensuing war which bears his name.

The strategy of the alliance is difficult to recover; one can only make inferences from what actually happened. Ptolemy sent a fleet under the command of Patroclus to the waters off Athens. We do not know the size or composition of the fleet. A base camp was set up on a small island opposite cape Sunium (Paus. 1.1.1 and 3.6.4; Strabo 9.21); it is a most inhospitable place and can have been chosen only because nothing else was possible. There is evidence for brief and small-scale Ptolemaic presence in various places in Attica, about what one would expect for foraging parties.[46] It would seem that this was a fleet prepared for a naval battle, not one designed to transport an army. The land action was apparently to be undertaken by King Areus of Sparta, who led an army toward the Corinthian isthmus, either to engage the Antigonid garrison there and remove it, or to aid Athens in the expected siege by Antigonus, or both. On his first attempt, he could not get past the garrison at Corinth and returned to Sparta (Paus. 3.6.4). Meanwhile, Antigonus did bring Athens under siege, and no relief was forthcoming from either Areus or Patroclus. In the course of the siege, Antigonid troops were also active in Attica and along the coast; Pausanias refers to an attack "with an army and a fleet" and "ravaging the countryside of Athens" (Paus. 1.1.1).

In the autumn of that year (264), Antigonus was faced with a revolt of his mercenaries, mostly Gauls, in the garrison at Megara. This was a convenient development for the allies, and whether Ptolemaic agents or those of Athens, Sparta, or other allies instigated the revolt is open to speculation; the Gauls were quite capable of revolting all by themselves. In any case, Antigonus was spread thin. He could not detach troops from Corinth to deal with the revolt, he had to raise the siege of Athens and deal with it personally. He made a truce with

47

the Athenians, who optimistically planted crops to be harvested the next spring. The revolt of the Gauls was suppressed, perhaps with a little difficulty.[47] In that same autumn, but more likely early in the following spring, Alexander of Epirus (son of Pyrrhus and current king of Epirus) invaded Macedonia, but he was repulsed by an army nominally in command of Demetrius II, who could not have been more than thirteen or fourteen years old (Justin 26.2.9–12). The personal presence of Antigonus was not required. It is easy enough to suspect that someone was trying very hard to distract Antigonus from the siege of Athens.

In the spring of 263, Antigonus resumed the siege of Athens and destroyed the crops before they could be harvested. Meanwhile, Areus had marched his army back to the Isthmus, and he was killed in the resulting battle. The army returned to Sparta (Justin 26.2; Trogus *Prol.* 26; Polyaen. 4.6.20; Frontinus 3.4.2). Patroclus was unable to accomplish anything further and withdrew. What he was trying to accomplish may be suggested by an isolated anecdote in Athenaeus (8.334), where it is reported that Patroclus had sent a gift to Antigonus consisting of a basket of fish and figs. It seemed a perplexing gift to those around him, but Antigonus understood its meaning and laughed. It was a taunt – the wealthy ate fish, the poor ate figs; to be wealthy (successful), he must control the sea. This was an attempt by Patroclus to goad him into a naval battle. Antigonus was not a gambler; at this point he had little to gain and much to lose from a naval battle. He wanted control of Greece. He had just proved that he already had that; he could lose it or weaken it by an unsuccessful naval battle. A victory at sea at this point would bring him nothing but prestige. He was willing to forego prestige for actual power.

One must wonder what the Ptolemaic fleet under Patroclus was doing while all this was going on? What could it have done?

An ancient naval ship was a weapons system whose primary function was to capture or sink other similar weapons systems, other ships. Although the larger ships could mount catapults and reach other ships with their missiles, naval "bombardment" of land installations was not effective, usual or expected. The propulsion source for a fighting ship was human muscle, a lot of it. Rowers were not usually trained combat soldiers, and what is more, they took up almost all the available space on the ship. There was room for only a small company of combat soldiers. An invasion force of combat troops could be transported on escorted merchant ships, but they were slow, vulnerable, expensive, and required a secure landing place. Ptolemy was not sending an invasion force to Greek waters; the land action was the responsibility of his allies on the scene. Athens, Sparta, and the other Greeks would be counted on to supply the infantry manpower; Ptolemy was sending naval forces which were designed to engage other naval forces, those of Antigonus. Antigonus did not cooperate; he generally kept his navy in port,[48] and in any case avoided engagement. The Ptolemaic fleet under Patroclus had little to do.

This war was decided on land. What could a naval battle have accomplished? In a purely military sense, nothing. Not territory; the winner does not maintain possession of the battlefield. Certainly not "control of the sea." This is difficult enough in the modern period, and something no ancient navy could seriously hope for. The ships were not built to withstand prolonged periods at sea, especially in heavy weather, and were too cramped to carry any but minimal provisions. The general practice was to beach the ships at night while the crew went ashore. The closest thing to "control of the sea" was the possession of a sufficient number of well-maintained ships and skilled crews to enable a fleet to put to sea quickly and meet any threat in its vicinity. The value of a strong fleet, and the value of a naval victory, was primarily *psychological*. And the importance of psychological victories (or defeats) should not be underestimated. The loser of a naval battle has lost expensive ships and valuable (perhaps irreplaceable) manpower. His remaining troops, friends, and allies are demoralized and full of despair. They fight less effectively. The winner has suffered fewer and more bearable economic losses, and his remaining troops, friends, and allies are inspired to new and greater efforts. They fight more effectively. A naval victory can alter the course of the war. This is equally true of a land battle, of course, but the effect is often greater for a naval battle because the economic and human losses are higher, and there are fewer eyewitnesses and the magnitude of the victory or defeat is easily exaggerated.

Ptolemy was the disturber of the *status quo* in the Chremonidean War. His intention was to engage Antigonus in a naval battle which, if he were victorious, would damage Antigonus militarily and especially politically, making the success of Ptolemy's Greek allies on land much more likely. If Ptolemy should lose (and consequently lose the war), he would have lost some ships and men, but the political situation in Greece would remain as it was. He had much to gain, little to lose.

The intention of Antigonus was merely to keep what he had. Aggressive moves to change the *status quo* could wait for a later time, if desired. To engage Ptolemy in a naval battle could gain him nothing except prestige; he could win the war on land in Greece without a naval battle, and he did. To engage in a naval battle and lose it could cost him the war on land. He had much to lose, and little to gain by a naval battle. And so, with the gift of a basket of fish and figs, Patroclus was trying, probably not for the first time, to goad him into staking all on a naval battle. The laughter of Antigonus is understandable as the expressed smile of self-satisfaction: he had a well-thought-out strategy, and it was working even better than he had hoped. Patroclus had been reduced to cute tricks.

Antigonus had spent much of his youth in Athens and was educated there. If he needed a precedent for his strategy, it was that of Pericles at the outset of the Peloponnesian War. Athens, weaker than Sparta on land, simply refused to engage the Spartans on land, but rather withdrew behind her walls and used her superior seapower to damage the Spartans. Sparta could not withstand Athens at sea. That Athens ultimately lost the war was not due to faulty strategy on Pericles' part. In just this way, with greater ultimate success, Antigonus engaged the forces of Ptolemy and his allies only where he was stronger – on land – and avoided a high-risk naval encounter. Ptolemy, in fact, had a similar plan – but it didn't work. His intention was to force Antigonus to meet him on his chosen field of battle, the sea, where he had a good chance of victory, and to avoid any encounter on land, where Antigonus was stronger. The chief difference, and an important one, is that Antigonus did have a naval force capable of meeting Ptolemy, but he chose not to use it on Ptolemy's terms. On the other hand, Ptolemy did not have an adequate land force with which to challenge Antigonus. He had no options.

One can marvel at the cynical way in which Ptolemy exploited Athens and Sparta and the other Greeks; he surely knew they were no match for the Macedonian army. The failure of his strategy cost him nothing, but it was very costly to the Greeks. It was a very efficient, cost-effective, and cautious strategy, one which minimized the possibility and costs of defeat. It was perhaps too cautious to make success likely; success depended on the cooperation of his adversary, Antigonus.

Ptolemy's caution was certainly a matter of strategy, and not a personality defect. It has been almost axiomatic in scholarly literature[49] to assume that Ptolemy Philadelphus was nearly incompetent in military matters and foreign affairs, that his sister/wife Arsinoë II was the brains behind the throne, most especially for this war, which went badly because she had died and Ptolemy did not implement her plans correctly. That Arsinoë was very clever and influential is not to be doubted; so were many other people, including other queens. That Philadelphus himself was interested in sensual pleasures and drinking is also not to be doubted; so were Philip II and Demetrius Poliorcetes, whose military acumen is legendary. Ptolemy Philadelphus did undertake bold action and had many successes during his long reign, before and after his marriage to Arsinoë;[50] perhaps some unknown advisors (even Arsinoë) are responsible for some of them, but in any case the king was responsible for accepting advice wisely or not, and should get full credit or blame. Ptolemy's low-risk strategy for the Chremonidean War may have been very sensible, if his war aims were limited. We don't know the causes of this war; the evidence simply doesn't exist. Several suggestions have been made,[51] and they can be divided into two categories: preventive war, against a perceived future threat from Antigonus, and opportunistic war, seizing an opportunity to weaken Antigonus. In either case, there was no immediate danger to Ptolemy from Antigonus; his war aims could have been limited. He could afford to follow a cautious strategy. He could afford to lose the war.

By the late summer of 263 (the beginning of the archonship of Antipater, Athenian archon year 263/2), Athens capitulated unconditionally. It was no doubt necessary to take some action against certain individuals. Chremonides had no difficulty escaping to Ptolemy, for whom he commanded a fleet some years later (Polyaen. V.18). The seer, antiquarian, and historian Philochorus was not so lucky; we learn that he was executed by Antigonus at the end of the war (Suidas, s.v. Philochorus). It is likely enough that there were other executions. Antigonus reinstalled a garrison on the Museum Hill inside the city, and announced that until further notice the internal government would be under his direction.[52] This was no doubt accomplished in what had become his usual manner: personal connections and relationships. He appointed individuals he thought he could trust as officials of the city. There was no need to rearrange the government at all; it was only necessary to assure that the usual officials were people he could trust. This followed the pattern of

Demetrius in earlier years (*c.* 294–287), and there is some evidence for it in the appointment of garrison commanders (discussed in the previous chapter). In some cases, election also took place, either before or after a nomination by Antigonus. The situation seems to have been very like the *commendatio* exercised by Augustus. It was not a constitutional matter at all, but a matter of personal authority (*auctoritas*), but not therefore less effective. At first this personal authority was reinforced by the presence of a garrison in the city, but eventually even that would not be necessary. The garrison was removed *c.* 255 BC, because it was no longer needed.[53]

Athens and Sparta and the other allies were pawns in the great game between Antigonus and Ptolemy. Antigonus won the Chremonidean War – against Athens and the Greek allies. Ptolemy had not yet been engaged.

The Chremonidean War was, after all, not simply a war between Antigonus and Athens; it was also a war between Antigonus and Ptolemy. It was for this reason as well that it was necessary for Antigonus to maintain a tight grip on Athens even after the city had been defeated. He was still at war with Ptolemy. He defeated the Ptolemaic fleet under Patroclus in a great naval battle off the island of Cos a short time later, in a situation where neither side had anything to gain or lose *except* prestige (and the ships and men, of course). The evidence for the Battle of Cos is even less than meager: Athenaeus (V.209e) expended many words describing famous big ships, and ended by telling his readers he would omit discussion of the ship of Antigonus, in which he defeated Ptolemy's generals off Cos and later dedicated the ship to Apollo. Diogenes Laertius, in his biographical sketch of the philosopher Arcesilaus (D.L.4.39), reports that Arcesilaus didn't flatter king Antigonus after the seafight off Cos, like other people did. And Plutarch (*Mor.* 545b) in an account of "Famous Sayings of Kings . . ." recounts how Antigonus II, in the seafight off Cos, responded to one of his companions who worried that they were outnumbered by suggesting that his presence counted for something. Thus, all we know is that there was a Battle of Cos between Antigonus and Ptolemy, Antigonus was outnumbered but he won, and he dedicated his flagship to Apollo. There is no way to establish a date for the battle with any certainty, but there is general agreement that it falls somewhere between 262 and 256 BC[54] It happened after the capitulation of Athens and the end of the Chremonidean War on the Greek mainland, and prior to a time of peace in the Aegean recorded for the year 255 in a Delian inscription (*I.G.* XI, 2, 116). This time of peace is subject to much interpretation and is hardly conclusive evidence, but it is the latest possible date in any case. The battle could not have taken place prior to the capitulation of Athens, and would very likely have taken place as soon as practical thereafter, surely within seven years. I suggest that Antigonus, at an opportune time after affairs on the mainland of Greece were securely in his control and he had nothing to lose, sought out the Ptolemaic fleet at a time and place of his choosing. He fought the naval battle at a time and place when he could afford to lose, as he clearly could not afford to lose while the Chremonidean War was still raging in Greece.

The relative chronology of the few known events is clear enough:

- tension between Ptolemy Philadelphus and Antigonus Gonatas, hostility in Athens toward Antigonus,
- the declaration of war by all the (now open) allies against Antigonus,
- the nearly simultaneous arrival of a Ptolemaic fleet under Patroclus in the Saronic Gulf, the unsuccessful assault on Corinth by a Spartan army under Areus, and Antigonid land and naval harassment of Attica,
- the siege of Athens by Antigonus,
- the distraction of Antigonus by a revolt of Gallic mercenaries at Megara and an invasion of Macedonia by Alexander of Epirus,
- the lifting of the siege of Athens under truce,
- the resumption of the siege of Athens, and another unsuccessful assault on Corinth by Areus and his death,
- the capitulation of Athens, and
- the withdrawal of Patroclus and the Ptolemaic fleet.

There was a hiatus of a few years in overt hostilities between Antigonus and Ptolemy, which flared anew when the Second Syrian War broke out. The primary antagonists in that conflict were Antiochus II and Ptolemy II Philadelphus. Antigonus, long on friendly terms with Antiochus, was not formally involved in the war but saw an opportunity to permanently weaken Ptolemy. The result was the Battle of Cos, a memorable naval victory for Antigonus. The Battle of Cos was the *coda* for the Chremonidean War.

7

AN OLD MAN'S
TROUBLES

The final decade and a half of the life of Antigonus Gonatas is, to us, nearly void of events and information. He was about sixty-five years old at the Battle of Cos *c*. 255, and for the remaining fifteen years of his life we know only that he endured the loss of his major garrison at Corinth to his nephew, Alexander the son of Craterus; he regained it a few years later by a trick; he lost it again, permanently, to Aratus of Sicyon, along with some other smaller garrisons, and in the meantime he fought a victorious naval battle against Ptolemy off Andros. We also know that his sister Stratonike, wife of Antiochus II, died and a festival was established at Delos in her honor.

It was probably in 253 that Antigonus created the "Stratonikeia" at Delos in honor of his sister, who had been a frequent visitor and dedicator to the shrines of Apollo and Artemis on the island. This need not have any political significance, and another festival instituted at about the same time, the "Antigoneia" is problematic as well. It was dedicated to Apollo, Artemis, and Leto, and it may be celebrating his recent victory at the naval Battle of Cos, which was of recent memory and known to all.[55] Its political significance, however, may just as easily be nothing more than a public demonstration of his piety.

Shortly thereafter, in or about the year 252 BC, Antigonus lost his garrisons at Corinth, Chalcis, and Eretria. The commander of the garrison at Corinth was Alexander, son of Craterus, hence nephew to Antigonus. He had succeeded his father in that position, but perhaps not directly. The latest mention of Craterus is in 271/0, when he led a force from Corinth to aid a tyrant at Elis (unsuccessfully). He would have been about fifty years old at the time. At some time between 270 and 252, Alexander became the garrison commander. One possible explanation for his "revolt" from his uncle is that he

54

was not awarded his father's position when Craterus died, but had to wait a few years. A possible interim commander would be the former "archpirate" Ameinias, who was a trusted confederate of Antigonus in 276 and had led a rescue mission to Sparta in 272, apparently on his own authority or at least with an independent command. There is no evidence to support this hypothesis, nor is there any evidence to indicate when Craterus died, when Alexander assumed command, or why he broke with Antigonus.[56]

Alexander proclaimed himself an independent king, of Corinth, Chalcis, and Eretria. These other two Antigonid garrisons had joined in his revolt. There is no evidence to suggest that Alexander, as commander of the Corinth garrison, also controlled Chalcis and Euboea; even the trusted Craterus does not seem to have exercised any control over those garrisons. Such control is not necessary to explain why they joined him; even if he had controlled them, his orders to the subordinate commanders could have easily been disobeyed in favor of their greater allegiance to king Antigonus. It is more likely that the individuals in charge of the garrisons at Chalcis and Eretria (we do not know their names) had been suborned by Alexander, and their troops followed their orders. It is tempting to see the hand of Ptolemy here; this would be a fine revenge for his defeat by Antigonus at the Battle of Cos. But there is no evidence for any involvement of Ptolemy, and if he had worked some persuasion (bribery?) on Alexander, the fact remains that Alexander was disaffected for some reason, and thus susceptible to the influence of Ptolemy.

It would have been a fine revenge, indeed, because what it cost Antigonus was much of his fleet. Corinth was an important naval base for Antigonus, although not the only one (he still had ships at Piraeus and at Demetrias, and probably other places as well). It certainly would have been possible for some of the ships, under the initiative of their own captains, to sail away from Corinth and join the Antigonid fleet elsewhere, just as the fleet of Demetrius after Ipsus either went over to Ptolemy, or back to Antigonus, apparently on the initiative of the individual captains. Perhaps many of the ships at Corinth did find their way back to Antigonus; this might explain why Antigonus took no immediate action against Alexander. It wasn't absolutely necessary.

Aratus of Sicyon probably had a role to play, but the sequence of events is unclear. Aratus gained control of Sicyon in 251/0, probably after the revolt of Alexander. Shortly afterward, Aratus made a voyage to Ptolemy to get money, which he succeeded in doing. He had earlier received generous gifts from Antigonus and the relationship between the two had been good, as had the relationship between Antigonus and Cleinias, father of Aratus. But that would change. Aratus made several attempts to dislodge Alexander from Corinth, and these attempts, whether done with the knowledge or consent of Antigonus or not, may explain the inaction of Antigonus: he would let Aratus try his hand first. These attempts ended abruptly when Alexander made an alliance with the Achaean League, of which Sicyon was also a member (Plut. *Arat.* 18.1).

In the meantime, Alexander attempted to add Athens to his new kingdom, but his invitation was refused and his subsequent forceful attempts were resisted by Athens, with the help of Aristomachos of Argos (a longtime ally of Antigonus). Athens and Argos eventually bought peace from Alexander, probably in 250/49, with Aristomachos providing the money (*I.G.* II², 774); the Piraeus garrison commander, Heracleitus, was also instrumental (*Syll.*³, 454).

Antigonus does not seem to have offered any direct help to Athens in this incident, and he never succeeded in dislodging Alexander from Corinth; so far as we know, he never tried. A shortage of manpower is a real possibility. Antigonus had always made much use of mercenaries. Indeed, there is no evidence for any general levy of troops in Macedonia at all; the wars of Alexander and the Successors had taken their toll on Macedonian manpower, and after a generation or two, Macedonians willing and able to soldier were in the employ of all of the hellenistic kings, not just the King of Macedonia. At about this time, Antigonus had been named guardian of two minor children of King Nicomedes of Bithynia, along with Ptolemy and several Ionian cities; Nicomedes wanted many disparate powers to guarantee the succession. His rejected son by a prior marriage, Ziaelas, immediately took up arms, requiring the guardians and guarantors to send troops against him (Memnon, *FGrH* 434, F14). Perhaps the mission to Bithynia and the loss of the manpower at Corinth reduced Antigonus to inaction, either because of lack of available additional manpower or lack of money to pay them.

After a few years (*c.* 247), Antigonus did manage to recover Corinth: by luck, cleverness, and exertion. Alexander died (we do not know how or exactly when) and his widow, Nicaea, maintained control of Corinth. Antigonus offered her a marriage to his son Demetrius, which she eagerly accepted. If it had happened, that marriage would have returned Corinth to Antigonid control, but it was not necessary. A festive wedding feast was held in the city of Corinth, and while everyone was well occupied in the revels, Antigonus took a small body of troops and marched up to the garrison on Acrocorinth. It was late at night, no one was expected, and when he knocked on the door, it was opened to him. Before anyone could consider who was supposed to be in charge, his troops had taken control (Plut. *Arat.* 17; Polyaen. 4.6.1). It is a long and steep climb, and Antigonus was over 70 years of age; whatever the cause of his inaction up to this point, it was not serious illness or weakness of age. The wedding did not, of course, take place and no more is heard of Nicaea.

The naval battle of Andros, another victory over Ptolemy, took place shortly afterward, in 246 or 245. There is general agreement on the date, because it is assumed the recovery of the naval base at Corinth is a precondition.[57] Trogus gives the name of the defeated Ptolemaic admiral, and Plutarch calls Antigonus "the old man" (*geron*) in this context, where he repeats the anecdote that Antigonus asserting that his own presence compensates for inferiority in numbers. The battle is here identified as Andros; in *Mor.* 545b, Plutarch tells the same story but identifies the battle as Cos. Another version of the story (*Mor.* 183c) does not name the naval battle. Obviously, the doublet casts doubt on the accuracy of the event, at least in its attribution to Cos or Andros. But both battles are named, and so they did occur and Antigonus was victorious and probably present at both (but probably did not say the same thing twice!). Antigonus celebrated this victory by instituting two more festivals at Delos, the "Soteria" and the "Paneia."[58]

It is deceptively simple to suggest that when Antigonus controlled Corinth, he had a strong navy, and without Corinth, he did not. The two may not be that closely related. The fact is that we do not know the size, the structure or the basing of the Antigonid fleet. We only know that he had one, and it was rather well known. Plutarch uses what appears to be a common phrase when he speaks of something so thoroughly dissolved that "even the Antigonid fleet could sail through it" (*Mor.* 1078c).

In any event, Antigonus did not keep Corinth for long. He lost it to Aratus of Sicyon in 243, in a surprise assault on the garrison in the darkness of night. Although he had some help from some of the mercenaries inside, it was a violent event; two of the most important officials in the garrison, Theophrastus and the philosopher Persaios, were killed.[59]

Immediately after gaining Corinth, Aratus arranged to bring the city into the Achaean League, and at the same time brought in Troezen, Epidaurus, and Megara.[60] No mention is made of Antigonid garrisons in this context; if he still maintained garrisons in Troezen and Megara, they would have been lost at this time. Aratus also attempted to persuade Athens to join the Achaean League, and followed up with an invasion of Attica. The invasion met with no success whatever and the effort was dropped (Plut. *Arat.* 24). Either Athens remained loyal to Antigonus, or the Antigonid forces in the Piraeus and subsidiary garrisons were adequate to the task, or both.

The relationship between Antigonus and Aratus was a stormy one. Antigonus had been on very friendly terms with Cleinias, the father of Aratus, and with Aratus as well at first. He was inclined to flatter Aratus publicly to win his favor, and probably gave him money on more than one occasion. Aratus sought money from Antigonus, and also from Ptolemy. It is likely enough that Antigonus did not give him as much money as he wanted, or that Ptolemy was more generous. The account of Plutarch is not always clear which "king" Aratus is importuning for money, but he certainly had dealings with both Antigonus and Ptolemy at one time or another (Plut. *Arat.* 2, 4, 11, 13, 15). Antigonus apparently lost the bidding war, and paid dearly for it. Corinth did not again hold an Antigonid garrison until Doson recovered it in 225/4.

Perhaps it did not matter much. The loss of Corinth and possibly other smaller garrisons failed to produce any grave consequences. Polybius insists that, probably about this time, Antigonus made a treaty with the Aetolians to partition the territory of the Achaean League (headed by Aratus).[61] If true, this agreement had no results. In fact, shortly before his death, Antigonus made a formal peace with the Achaean League (Plut. *Arat.* 33).

Antigonus Gonatas died in 240/39 BC at about eighty years of age. We have no record of the circumstances of his death and the date must be deduced from the reign of his son, Demetrius II.[62] Demetrius was in his mid-thirties, mature, experienced, and ready to assume the burden of kingship, the "glorious servitude," as Antigonus had described it (Aelian, *VH* 2.20).

8

THE NATURE OF THE MONARCHY

We who live in modern constitutional democracies are constantly aware of the limitations and circumscription of the powers exercised by political officials and institutions. It would be gratifying to us and fully in accord with our traditional thought-processes to be able to make a list of those powers and prerogatives which a Macedonian king possessed and did not possess. Such an attempt is futile, however. Macedonians and Greeks of the third century BC did not think exactly as we do. Such evidence as exists clearly suggests that the *potential* power of the king of Macedonia was absolute, but his *actual* power was fluid and depended upon the political realities of the moment. The conclusion of Ernst Badian is apt: "the king . . . had precisely what rights and powers [he] could get away with."[63]

There were no constitutional restraints on Antigonus. Although he no doubt consulted with close friends and associates from time to time, there was no organized "Council of Friends." Some Macedonian kings found it desirable or expedient to convene the army in assembly; there is no evidence that Antigonus ever did, nor was he or any Macedonian king required to do so.[64] Indeed, for Antigonus Gonatas it would not have been possible, since he never had a standing citizen army. He made extensive use of mercenaries and any Macedonian subjects were volunteers serving for pay. The composition and size of his military and naval force varied with need and availability. The previous discussion of known garrison commanders (Chapter 5) makes this clear: Craterus, his half-brother who was in command at Corinth, was a Macedonian; Ameinias the archpirate who had some position at Corinth was probably a Phocian; Hierocles at the Piraeus was a Carian; Heracleitus who succeeded Hierocles at the Piraeus was an Athenian.

Antigonus surely needed to appoint officials to assist him in the administration of Macedonia: absolute power or not, he could not take care of everything himself. The evidence suggests that such appointments were on an *ad hoc* basis and a formal title was not necessary. One example is an inscription (*Syll.*[3], 459) from Berea which is dated by the thirty-sixth year of the reign of Antigonus (probably 248/7). It contains a letter from Demetrius to Harpalus; neither man is identified by title. Demetrius rather curtly writes to Harpalus that he has learned that some temple revenues have been diverted to political use; Harpalus is instructed (the imperative is used) to see to it that the revenues are returned to the temple. The Demetrius of this inscription is certainly the son of Antigonus, the future Demetrius II. He doesn't need a title. Harpalus obviously has the authority and power to do what is demanded of him; he is some kind of official in the city of Berea or the region, but no title is used. He knew what his job was, and so, presumably, did everyone else concerned.

The status of cities and regions within Macedonia was variable, depending in large part on the traditions of the city or perhaps its relationship to the king. Evidence is meager, but the variability is demonstrated by a series of inscriptions from the island of Cos, dated to 242/1.[65] The Coans are seeking grants of asylum to the temple of Asclepius on Cos, and what they have in common is that all express goodwill between the individual cities and Cos, and between king Antigonus and Cos. The four cities are Cassandreia, Amphipolis, Philippi, and Pella. They are four major cities in Macedonia, not far apart, but they are not governed the same way. Each awarded the grant of asylum: Cassandreia passed a decree in the *boule*; Philippi passed a decree in the *ekklesia*; and Amphipolis and Pella simply issued the decree by "the city of ...." The internal governing structure is obviously not identical.

Macedonia had not been an urban culture, and this did not change under Antigonus. The larger cities were earlier Greek colonies which had become part of Macedonia during the reign of Philip II. Some cities established by kings (Philippi, Thessaloniki, Cassandreia) would eventually become important at a later date, but in the third century they were not major urban centers of the Greek-speaking world. Antigonus is believed to have founded at least three cities, all named Antigoneia: on the Axius river in Paonia (Pliny, *N.H.* 4.10.17), on the Aous river in Atintania (Pliny, *N.H.* 4.1.1), and in Chalcidice (Livy 44.10), but none of them became cities of any importance and their locations are quite uncertain.[66] They may have been not much more than garrison towns, designed as a permanent presence against northern tribes.

Some cities in Macedonia may have had a democratic *polis* form of government for their internal affairs, others may have had an individual (or several of them) appointed by the king to administer their affairs, but there is no evidence for any consistency, and no *epistates* of a city as in later Ptolemaic Egypt.[67] It must be noted that *epistates*, like *epimeletes* or *strategos*, common word is a in Greek, often merely descriptive of a function and not necessarily a title. When they do become titles, the actual meaning can vary from one time and place to another. The earliest reference to any *epistates* or *hypepistates* in Macedonia is *I.G.*, 2, 1.1028 from Thessaloniki, dated to the reign of Demetrius II, *c.* 230 BC, and *I.G.*, 2, 1.2 from the same city during the reign of Antigonus Doson, *c.* 224/3. These are apparently minor officials.

There is a relatively plentiful supply of evidence for a *strategos*, if the term is taken to mean simply someone who commands troops. But an individual who is called *strategos* does not, because of that descriptive title, function as a provincial or regional governor. The power and authority of the individual depended on that individual's relationship to the king and the king's needs at the time.[68]

For several reasons, one should not expect the same complexity of government in Antigonid Macedonia as in the contemporary hellenistic monarchies to the east. While the cosmopolitan nature of the hellenistic world does suggest that regional differences would eventually diminish, the differences were still profound during the reign of Gonatas. Even if one assumes that the rulers of the three major kingdoms held similar ideas of government (a dubious assumption), they were faced with three very different bodies of tradition on which to impose those ideas. It would take some time before the convergence of practice would be apparent. In fact, similarities do begin to appear by the late third century BC, a few generations after the unifying conquest of Alexander. But the reign of Gonatas is too early to expect successful imitation of or agreement with the more complex eastern governments. Antigonus Gonatas was very likely unable to impose any rigid organization on his governmental structure, and may have been unwilling to do so.

Although Antigonus can be said to have governed, after a fashion, from 283 onward, he did not have any significant control until after the battle of Lysimacheia in 277. Only a few years later he lost control temporarily to Pyrrhus. He recovered Macedonia by *c.* 272 at the latest, but any attention he might have given to internal administration was soon diverted by the tensions leading to the outbreak of the Chremonidean War, which was a direct challenge to his international position. Throughout this period he had to attend to affairs in Greece; it was necessary to establish his relationship with the various Greek cities. Only after c. 250 would he have had the leisure to organize his internal administration systematically, if indeed he was ever inclined to do so. At that point it must have occurred to him that he had already been governing for about thirty years without any clear organized system and there was no urgent need to change things. The flexibility which he had practiced out of necessity at first may, in the end, have been desirable.

The power of Antigonus as king was largely personal. His personal popularity was all-important, and his personal relationship with subordinates was crucial. The king necessarily delegated authority to others, who rarely had a fixed title, and the limits of their authority were likewise not clearly stated. The overriding authority of the king himself may have been the only effective limit. The relationship between the king and his subordinates was one of personal trust. The king chose individuals to govern or exercise the necessary authority in his name and simply trusted them to do it (whatever "it" was). Since the king was, by definition, the most powerful man in Macedonia, violation of that trust could have grave consequences, a fact known to all. The kingship of Macedonia, and especially in the reign of Gonatas, rested on minimal legal foundations; the successful king of Macedonia was essentially a masterful politician.

Some movement toward a systematic, well-defined, internal organization may have begun in the reign of his son and successor, Demetrius II, although specific evidence is lacking. There are traces of more organized administration under Antigonus III Doson, and under Philip V Macedonia is governed not too differently in principle from the Seleucid and Ptolemaic realms.

Doson had not only the stability of fifty years of Antigonid rule over Macedonia, which provided comfortable circumstances in which to bring about a careful reorganization of government, he also had a strong motivation to do so. He came to power as regent for the young Philip V, and knew all along that fate could make Philip a king while very young. Philip would need all the help he could get from a strong, reliable, and consistent internal organization of officials – something which had not heretofore been necessary. On the contrary, Antigonus Gonatas was a man of mature years and judgment when he became king; if, early in his reign, he was concerned about the succession of his son at a tender age, competent regents were at hand in the persons of his half-brothers Craterus and Demetrius the Fair. Antigonus did not die too soon; Demetrius II was over thirty years of age on his accession and had the added advantage of experience for many years with his father. He, too, had an available regent for his young son in the person of his cousin Antigonus Doson, a man of mature years and wide experience. Doson did serve as regent for Philip, the son of Demetrius. Eventually he became king in his own name, but as caretaker pending Philip's maturity. In the event of his death prior to Philip's coming of age, there was for the first time in Antigonid history no close male relative standing by ready to assist a young king. It was a new problem, requiring a new solution: strong organization. For a strong king with mature judgment, flexibility and informality could be advantageous, often desirable. For a young and inexperienced king, the same situation could be dangerous. Thus, it was only late in the reign of Doson that the Macedonian structure of government began to parallel the more rigid and complex bureaucracies of the Ptolemies and Seleucids.

The same situation can be seen in the relationship of Antigonus to the Greek cities. The relationship was not formal; it was not spelled out in detail by formal treaty or edict of the king. Rather, the king seems to have undertaken considerable effort to cultivate close personal relationships with important politicians in Athens, in Argos, and he attempted to do as much with Aratus of Sicyon. We have no evidence for the relationship of the king to individuals in Corinth, although one must suspect something similar took place.

Antigonus governed in Macedonia and exercised a hegemony in Greece primarily through personal connections. He relied on his friends and associates to act in his interests. There was little practical difference whether the individuals involved were Macedonians or natives of a Greek city. The tyrants at Argos during most of his reign governed in his interests because it was also in their interest. Athenian politicians, especially after 255 BC, were no doubt patriotic Athenians, but were also friends or adherents of Antigonus and effectively governed in his interest. The trusted subordinates who were Macedonians also could function more or less autonomously, but in the interests of the king. His half-brother Craterus was involved in the ransom of Mithres with apparent full power to negotiate, but there was no doubt he was acting on behalf of Antigonus. The same man led a relief force (unsuccessfully) to aid the tyrant of Elis without any apparent involvement of Antigonus. Heracleitus (an Athenian), the commander of the Piraeus garrison, energetically defended both his Macedonian garrison and the city of Athens against the attacks of Alexander, son of Craterus. Alexander's successful revolt is an indication of how complete was the trust between Antigonus and his subordinates. Had there been a rigid chain of command, known limits to the power of the subordinate, or any kind of "checks and balances" in the system at all, the revolt of Alexander may not have been possible.

Under the circumstances, the success of Antigonus depended on how well he chose good men to assist him in exercising his power. The revolt of Alexander must be counted as a failure on the part of Antigonus. He also seems to have experienced some failures in Athens in the years immediately preceding the Chremonidean War. On balance, however, he was rather successful in maintaining power for forty years, a power which ultimately depended on personal relationships.

One cannot overlook the possible influence on Antigonus of his father. Demetrius Poliorcetes was a Macedonian and operated within this same Macedonian tradition; yet he was more likely than most to defy tradition where it suited his purposes. Despite some ideological flirtations, Demetrius was basically a very practical man, and so was his son. Demetrius developed an admiration and understanding of the Greek *polis* traditions, especially those of Athens, and he arranged for his son to be educated in the philosophical schools at Athens. As a result, Antigonus Gonatas may have had a greater understanding of the Greeks than any other Macedonian king, in or out of Macedonia. Also, Demetrius had always looked to greater things than Macedonia. Although Gonatas was considerably less ambitious than his father, he had a broad vision of Macedonia and its position in the international arena.

The Greek political tradition had much in common with the Macedonian tradition. Notwithstanding the Greek (especially Athenian) emphasis on the supremacy of law and of institutions, political power was still essentially personal. Political and social connections mattered very much for one who chose to hold political power within the legal framework, and an individual was held personally accountable for his actions. Political failure could have social as well as legal consequences. In his relationship with Athens, for example, Antigonus could follow the Macedonian tradition of personal political connections, while leaving the legal and institutional formalities to his Athenian friends.

The cherished autonomy of the Greek *polis* was something well understood by Antigonus, who was content to honor that tradition so long as in so doing he did not violate his own necessary primary goals. Except for the period immediately following the Chremonidean War in Athens, the cities of Greece appeared to function as sovereign states, with the implied provision that they must not work contrary to the interests of Antigonus.

Edward Luttwak, in describing the Roman empire under the Julio–Claudians,[69] has written:

"The control mechanism was complex ... always there was the latent threat of force ... By channeling money and favors through chosen client chiefs, the Romans helped the latter gain power over their subjects, while the Romans gained power over them" (pp. 36–7), and

"The rulers of eastern client states and their subjects did not actually have to *see* Roman legions marching toward their cities in order to respond to Rome's commands ..." (p. 32).

Antigonus followed a similar practice. His strategically located garrisons were sufficient reminders of the "latent threat of force" but not nearly adequate to actually maintain control by force. For the most part, it was not necessary to "actually have to *see*" his military force to believe that it would be used, and used effectively.

"The stability of the system requires a constant diplomatic effort" (Luttwak, 1976, p. 192). One need not doubt that the hegemony of Greece required a similar constant diplomatic effort from Gonatas. The most conspicuous failure was the Chremonidean War, resulting in the only instance wherein the Greek cities did actually see his military force used against them. On the one hand, any resort to military force can be seen as a failure of diplomatic activity. On the other hand, the fact that it was necessary only once in forty years, and that it was successful, indicates that the policy on balance was successful.

Walter Lacquer offered his analysis of a similar kind of hegemony in the modern world.[70] He observed that the Soviet Union exerted an influence over neighboring Finland in which the threat of force was not at all obvious, but in which certain understandings prevailed, including that "only those political parties approved by the Soviet Union can participate in the government" of the sovereign nation of Finland, and that "the Finns are supposed to exert self-censorship" (Laquer, 1977, p. 38). A similar situation prevailed for Antigonus

Gonatas in third-century Greece, most notably Athens after 255 BC (but also earlier, and especially while Demetrius was king of Macedonia). The approval of the king, of course, was not formal and generally not publicly admitted or announced; "it is part of the whole process to deny its very existence." (Lacquer, 1977, p. 38). The maintenance of the fiction of the complete independence of the Greek cities was both necessary and desirable. First, the tradition of independence was profoundly felt, and any violation would at a minimum nullify any support the king might receive from individuals within the cities. Second, internal opposition or outside agitation was minimized by the simple fact that it is difficult to liberate that which is already free. Opponents of Gonatas had first to convince the citizens that they needed liberating. The deliberately imprecise and informal nature of the hegemony enhanced its effectiveness and minimized the dangers to it.

Greece was a buffer state for Macedonia against Ptolemy – or any other potential threat from the south or east – in the same way that Macedonia served as a buffer for Greece against the barbarians to the north. By thus defending Greece (through fortifications and political control), he also defended Macedonia. It was the ambition of Antigonus to secure Macedonia and to exercise a preponderant influence in Greece. He never attempted outright conquest of Greece, perhaps because he was unable to do so, but it is also true that the subjugation of Greece was neither necessary nor desirable. Antigonus governed in the Macedonian tradition, and the autonomy allowed to Greek cities was probably not significantly greater than the local autonomy customary in Macedonia. Macedonian government was traditionally autocratic, but not totalitarian.

An ill-defined hegemony of Greece was effective; there were no obvious reliable alternatives. Subjugation and incorporation of Greece into his kingdom would have been very costly in time and resources and, given the Greek traditions of independence, ultimate success was by no means assured. To pursue no involvement whatsoever and allow the Greeks complete freedom of action was to invite disaster. Antigonus understood well the instability of Greek politics; it was safer to attempt to manipulate Greek political life than to remain apart from it and become a victim of someone else's manipulation. The issue could not be considered in a vacuum: Antigonus inherited his position from Demetrius, who had been fully involved in Greece. The king of Macedonia had been involved in Greek affairs for several generations, since the time of Philip II, whose policies and practices were very much like those employed by Antigonus. He had to deal with the world as he found it. For him to abandon his possessions and his role in Greek political life would have been seen as a sign of weakness by many and his tenure of Macedonia itself would not long survive such an abdication of power. If he had been inclined toward creative statecraft, to the establishment of some kind of confederacy with the Greek cities, there was no time for it.

His position as king of Macedonia was somewhat more secure because he had arguably inherited the position, but it required continued political and social skills. The Greek hegemony depended almost entirely on his personal relationships with individuals. A display of military force (garrisons) was necessary, but was not the essential component. Under the circumstances, the degree of success is impressive.

The political career of Antigonus Gonatas calls to mind another, better-known individual: Octavian, later known as Augustus. The young Octavian studied in Greece and, like most Roman aristocrats of the late Republic, he was familiar with the history of hellenistic kings. Perhaps he saw patterns worth emulating in Antigonus. Like Antigonus, he had a "father" (by adoption, Caesar) who had reached the pinnacle of power but was removed from it, at least partly because he had exercised that power too obviously. He, too, would have to deal with those who resented any infringement on their freedom, even though they saw his overwhelming power. Augustus allowed the Roman Republic to function, or appear to do so, just as Antigonus allowed the Greek cities to remain free and self-governing, or appear to be so. Both continued to maintain an adequate, if not too visible, military and naval force. Both created a system over the course of four decades which endured for more than a century.

9

THE MAN AND
THE KING

What can one know about Antigonus, the man? He has left us no scrapbook, no official records, and no lengthy memoirs. Even if he had, we might be well advised to consider it carefully, since such things do not always tell a full and accurate story. We have anecdotal glimpses of the man, and any conclusions must be very tentative.

What did he look like? Plutarch tells us (*Mor.* 458F) only that he was relatively ugly, in contrast to his famously handsome father. He is supposed to have resembled the god Pan, whose image graced some of his coins, and a small bronze bust may be a likeness of him, but this is uncertain.[71] The face has "large protruding ears and a pair of outwardly turned horns [which] produce a wild terror-striking face with swollen eyebrows and a flattened hawk's nose."[72] His allegiance to the god Pan may have begun with his victory over the Gauls at Lysimacheia, or after his victory in the Battle of Cos, or have predated both; the coins cannot be dated with sufficient accuracy. One of the several festivals he established at Delos was in honor of the god Pan.

How did he live? Again, no specific information is available, although the general accoutrements of the good life (clothing, buildings, implements) in the third century BC are rather well understood, and should be assumed. Archaeological investigation in Macedonia is relatively young, and the surface remains of buildings are few and in a state of nearly complete ruin (there is nothing comparable to, for example, the Parthenon in Athens). The locations of Demetrias, Pella, and Aegae (Vergina) are known; portions of fortification walls remain at Demetrias, as well as foundations of a few structures, including one identified as the probable "palace;" a palace site has been identified at Pella and at Vergina, this last probably built during the reign of Antigonus.[73] He no doubt spent some time at all of these places, as well as at Corinth and Athens but, as indicated earlier, we can rarely determine where he was residing at any particular point in time, nor how long he remained in that place. If he had a "capital city" at all, it was probably Demetrias, although the traditional royal residence of Pella would be very important. Aegae (Vergina) seems to have been something of a "summer palace" and religious and cultural center; the royal tombs of Macedonian kings were located there. Macedonia was not an urban culture, and Macedonian kings, especially the first and second generation after Alexander, were not *territorial* kings: they were not kings *of* a defined territory, and not even necessarily of a defined ethnic group of people; they were simply "kings" whose territory and subjects were somewhat variable. This is most true of the Seleucid empire. What was Seleucus king of? "Asia"? "Syria"? Both terms were used. It is somewhat less true of Ptolemy because Egypt was a rather well defined entity. But the Ptolemies always controlled some territory outside of Egypt as well. Macedonia was also a known location and people, but where were the borders? It is not possible for us to know, and it is quite possible that Antigonus himself did not always know either. Certainly some of the inhabitants were not "Macedonians" in the ethnic or linguistic sense, for example, in the Greek coastal cities.

For such a non-territorial king, it is probably misleading to speak of a "capital city" at all. He lived wherever he wanted to at the moment and his administrative staff, such as it was, either followed him around or could be located anywhere and everywhere, no doubt some of each.

But that is not to say Antigonus was a semi-nomadic barbarian. On the contrary, he was obviously an educated man with an appreciation of high culture. He had no need to establish an intellectual and artistic center, as did the Ptolemies at Alexandria or the Attalids later at Pergamum. It already existed in Athens, which was under his hegemony, but not only at Athens. Macedonian kings before him had brought poets and artists to Macedonia, and Tarn devoted a chapter[74] to identifying the various poets, historians, and philosophers who at one time or another made Macedonia their residence during the reign of Antigonus. Among the more permanent residents were the aged historian Hieronymus of Cardia, who had been associated with the Antigonids for three generations and wrote his history early in the reign of Antigonus (which unfortunately survives only in fragments of Diodorus), and the poet Aratus of Soli, who wrote a bridal hymn for Antigonus and Phila and may have written his *Phaenomena* at the specific request of Antigonus. The association of Antigonus with many of the philosophers of his time is well known and has already been mentioned. The religious envoys which had been sent to all the hellenistic kings by the Indian king Asoka, recently converted to Buddhism, had their best chance of a serious and cordial reception at the court of Antigonus.[75]

His interest in the life of the mind and his intellectual capacity for it are not in doubt. Had he been born into different circumstances, Antigonus might have been one of history's intellectuals, but he became a king instead. Though we can glimpse his character only from anecdotes, they all reveal a man who was practical, confident, disciplined, and even witty, as well as intelligent. Plutarch (*Mor.* 545b) called him ἄτυφος καὶ μέτριος: a man of no illusions and moderate in his thinking.

He had the intelligence to take advantage of opportunities, and to make his own opportunities, a strategic vision which developed and maintained a functioning monarchy in Macedonia and a hegemony in Greece for forty years with minimum cost in resources and manpower. His strategy during the Chremonidean War was very clever; had he been a little more clever, there may have been no Chremonidean War. His ruse to recover Corinth from the widow of Alexander, son of Craterus, was also clever; had he been more clever, he might not have lost Corinth to Alexander.

The frequent anecdotes about his parties remind us that he was very human, much more than the quiet intellectual. The anecdotes are all, of course, in later sources, but it is worth noting that this is the kind of image of the man which survived the years. Part of the ruse to recover Corinth from Nicaea was the lavishness of the banquet, and it seems not unexpected of him; Zeno referred to his noisy parties, and in the brief life of Arcesilaus, Diogenes Laertius (D.L.4.41) tells of a birthday party for Halkyoneus, his illegitimate son, for which Antigonus spent an astounding amount of money. He was a generous man; he was more generous than would be expected with an illegitimate son, and he gave gifts, including money, to many of his friends – for example, 3,000 drachma to the philosopher Cleanthes (D.L. 7.169) – and this seems to have been typical.

He had a sardonic sense of humor and most especially had the ability to laugh at himself and his condition. In the midst of the Chremonidean War, when the outcome was uncertain, he could laugh at the teasing gift of fish and figs from Patroclus. At another time (uncertain), when reminded that the other kings called themselves gods and asked why he did not do likewise, he responded that the man who carried his chamber pot knew he was no god (Plut. *Mor.* 360c–d). We are told that he called the diadem (a strip of linen worn around the king's head) a ῥάκος, a mere "rag," and that he considered monarchy "a glorious servitude" (ἐνδόξα δουλεία; Aelian 2.20).

Stoic philosophy would have been very helpful, because when one steps back to look at the whole life, Antigonus experienced at least as much volatility and change of fortune as did his more famous father, perhaps more so. The following chart, which necessarily double-counts some experiences shared by father and son, reveals the major successes and reverses of each. The numbers are not surprisingly greater for Antigonus, since they are the sum of events covering nearly fifty years, whereas those for Demetrius cover about thirty years.

		DEMETRIUS I		ANTIGONUS II	
		Successes	*Reverses*	*Successes*	*Reverses*
312	Gaza	x			
306	Salamis	x			
306	Athens	x			
301	Ipsus		x		x
295	king of Macedonia	x		x	
287	expulsion, revolt of Athens		x		x
283	failure of Asian expedition, death of Demetrius		x		x
277	Lysimacheia, king of Macedonia			x	
274	defeat by Pyrrhus				x
272	death of Pyrrhus			x	
265	Chremonidean War begins				x
262	victory in Chremonidean War			x	
255	victory at Cos			x	
252	loss of Corinth				x
249	recovery of Corinth			x	
247	battle of Andros			x	
243	loss of Corinth				x
	Totals	4	3	7	7
	(Antigonus alone)			6	4

Antigonus lived a long and eventful life. The accomplishments were considerable. He created a stable monarchy which would endure for a century; indeed, the last Antigonid king of Macedonia, Perseus, was removed by force of Roman arms and not by internal weakness. He established his Macedonia as a "great power" in hellenistic geopolitics, a position which it retained for the remainder of its existence, and which was not inevitable. The chaos in the 280s, before his victory at Lysimacheia, could have resulted in an insignificant peripheral Macedonia similar to its status prior to Philip II. The personal efforts and decisions of Antigonus II Gonatas created hellenistic Macedonia.

NOTES

1 It could mean "knockkneed" or something else about his knees, but no etymology seems satisfactory. For full discussion see E.L. Brown, "Antigonus Surnamed Gonatas."
2 D.L. 7.169; 9.110; 2.141; 7.6; 7.36; 4.41.
3 When Zeno died in 261, it was at the specific request of Antigonus that Athens passed a decree in his honor (D.L. 7.11).
4 Paus. 2.8.4; 7.8.3; Plut. *Arat.* 18.1; Polyaen. 6.5.
5 Plut. *Dem.* 8, 14–16, 21; D.S. 20.45–52, 82–88, 91–100.
6 Plut. *Pyrr.* 4. It is unlikely that Antigonus was present at Ipsus for two reasons. First, Demetrius no doubt would want to leave someone of authority and status in charge of his affairs in Greece during his absence; although very young, Antigonus possessed the requisite status for the job. Second, Plutarch's reference to Antigonus as a *meirakion*, a very young man, when describing events six or seven years later, probably indicates that in 301 Antigonus was not battle-seasoned, and Ipsus was sure to be a major battle. Antigonus would be of little use. We can only speculate whether anyone thought of the wisdom of not having three generations of an allegedly royal family present at one battle; it certainly would not have been a good idea. Antigonus the grandfather and Demetrius the father were quite enough to risk in one battle. The silence of our sources suggests that even if Antigonus were present, he played no major role. Indeed, Plutarch had two opportunities to mention Antigonus at Ipsus and failed to do so (the life of Demetrius and that of Pyrrhus).

7 J. Gabbert, "Pragmatic Democracy in Hellenistic Athens."
8 *I.G.* II² 682; Plut. *Mor.* 851,d-f; Paus. 1.26.3.
9 J. Seibert, *Historische Beiträge zu den dynastischen Verbindungen in hellenistischer Zeit*, G.M. Cohen, "The Marriage of Lysimachus and Nicaea," p. 354.
10 Paus. 1.26.3 lists four specific activities for which Olympiodorus was honored, and it has been difficult to place these in their correct context.

Opinions vary: see T.L. Shear, "Kallias of Sphettos and the Revolt of Athens in 286 BC," for full discussion and bibliography, where the recovery of the Piraeus by Olympiodorus is placed in 281/0 (pp. 26–9, n. 62). I have dealt with the career of Olympiodorus in "The Career of Olympiodorus of Athens (c. 340–270 BC)." *AncW* 27 (1996), 59–66.

11 The capture of the Piraeus by Olympiodorus is placed elsewhere by many scholars, but this conclusion also has support, most recently from Bengtson, *Die Diadochen* ... pp. 110ff. See Shear, op. cit. p. 52, n. 144 for earlier bibliography.

12 Plut. *Dem.* 44–46; *Mor.* 851; *I.G.* II², 682, 649, 389, 666, 667; Shear, op. cit.; Agora I, 7295; Paus. 1.26.1. Shear's monograph is a thorough, well-documented discussion of all relevant evidence. One might not accept all of his conclusions, yet the permanent value to scholarship of this *magnum opus* is obvious.

13 Kallias decree (Agora I, 7295), lines 13, 14.

14 Shear, op cit., p. 76, with citations of all the evidence.

15 Sextus Empiricus, *Adv. gramm.* 276, records an incident involving Sostratus, sent from Ptolemy, reciting a few lines from Homer to "Antigonus." H. Heinen, "Untersuchungen zur hellenistischen Geschichte des 3. Jahrhunderts v. Chr.," pp. 196–7 considers this an allusion to the naval battle of Cos shortly after the Chremonidean War, which dates the event much later. This allusion is not obvious, however, and this reference might mean that Sostratus, representing Ptolemy for the negotiations in Athens in 287/6, is dealing with Antigonus Gonatas who is representing his father Demetrius.

16 For full discussion, see Shear, op. cit., *passim*. The sticking point is a brief commentary by the later traveler Pausanias who reports the inscription on a statue base dedicated to Olympiodorus. Olympiodorus was honored for doing four things. One of the activities of Olympiodorus clearly refers to activity against Cassander at an earlier date. Another refers to a rescue of Eleusis, which probably also dates to the reign of Cassander, but could be contemporary with other events. The greatest achievement of Olympiodorus is said to have been his storming of the Museum Hill in Athens and driving out the Macedonians, and this was done with a small force of old men and youngsters. The second greatest event was his recovery of the Piraeus garrison. Shear, op. cit., pp. 11, 12, and Christian Habicht, *Untersuchungen zur politischen Geschichte Athens im 3. Jahrhundert v. Chr.*, p. 61, and others are very inclined to put the expulsion of the Macedonian garrison from the Museum Hill in this particular situation. The recovery of the Piraeus garrison is the most difficult, but may be associated with an earlier action against Cassander (Habicht, pp. 95–112, Paus. 101). But see above, where I have associated it with the expulsion of Lachares. Another relevant piece of information is the decree for the mercenary Strombichus (*I.G.* II², 667). He is honored and given Athenian citizenship in 266/5 because at some earlier time he had thrown in his lot with the Athenians and assisted in storming the Macedonian garrison on the Museum Hill, in which he had previously been second in command. That activity can also be associated with this revolt. It explains why Olympiodorus could storm the garrison with a small force of old men and

boys; he had the assistance of some of the Macedonian mercenaries themselves. However, it is not a certainty that the Museum Hill was taken by the Athenians at this time. The decree honoring Kallias indicates that at the time of his action against Demetrius, "the fort on the Mouseion was still occupied" (line 13, Shear's translation). This decree was passed a full sixteen years later, at which time it would certainly be appropriate to mention a very important event like the expulsion of the garrison in the Museum, if it had occurred later in connection with Kallias' activity at all. The end of the revolt of Athens was negotiated through the influence of the philosopher Crates, and Demetrius sailed off to Asia, the Ptolemaic fleet went home, and King Pyrrhus, who had been summoned by the Athenians to aid them against a siege by Demetrius, arrived too late to do anything except warn the Athenians to never again allow a king in their city. This revolt seems not to have accomplished much at all, perhaps partly *because* Demetrius still had a garrison within the city. Justin found no need to mention it in his very summary account, and in two biographies of Hellenistic kings, Plutarch says almost nothing about it. Indeed, Plutarch indicates in his *Life* of Demetrius (*Dem.* 51) that when Demetrius was captured by Seleucus he sent a message to his son and to commanders and friends in Athens and in Corinth that they should consider him dead. If we are to believe Plutarch, Demetrius still considered Athens very much under his control or influence. And in his account of the entire episode in his *Life* of Pyrrhus (*Pyrr.* 12), Plutarch says nothing at all about the revolution in Athens, merely that Pyrrhus visited the city in order to perhaps hinder the growing power of Demetrius. As will be seen, a likely occasion for the betrayal by Strombichus and the storming of the Museum garrison is the time when news reached Athens of the death of Demetrius, in late 283 or early 282 BC. For full discussion, see Gabbert, "The Career of Olympiodorus." *AncW* 27 (1996), 59–66.

17 *PHerc.* 339, col. v; see also Shear, op. cit., p. 29, n. 61.
18 Dittenberger, *Syll.*[3] 459, an inscription from Berea dated in the thirty-sixth year of King Antigonus; see also L. Robert, *REG* 64 (1951), 171–173 and M. Chambers, "The First Regnal Year of Antigonus Gonatas," p. 390.

NOTES TO PAGES 21–32

19 For a full discussion of events and complete citation of sources, see Chapter 11, "The Years of Chaos" and relevant appendices in Hammond and Walbank's *A History of Macedonia*, volume III. Of course, many of the conclusions remain arguable.
20 Memnon, *FGrH* F8, 3b; Justin 24.1.
21 This event is placed in 285 by Shear, op cit., p. 83.
22 Justin 24.1, "almost all" (*omnes ferme*) of the Greek cities were at war with Antigonus, but made war against him indirectly by attacking his allies, the Aetolians.
23 Paus. 4.5.4; Justin 25.2.
24 Paus. 1.4.3, 10.20.5, 22.12.

25 *Syll.*³, 454, line 7, "and has now been appointed by the king as general (*strategos*) of the Piraeus and of the other places organized with (*tattomenon*) the Piraeus." This certainly includes Salamis, where the inscription was found, and probably Sunium and Rhamnous.

26 Polyaen. 4.6.18; Trogus, *Prol.* 25.

27 Peace with Antiochus, Justin 25.1. The evidence for this marriage is scattered and largely inferential. The poet Aratus of Soli apparently wrote a hymn to celebrate the wedding; Phila, like her mother, was a frequent visitor and dedicator to the sanctuary of Apollo at Delos. For fuller discussion, see Tarn, *Antigonos Gonatas*, pp. 174, 226–227, 350; Peter Green, *Alexander to Actium*, pp. 141–143; and *CAH* 7, 203 ff.

28 Plut. *Pyrr.* 26.7. Some of the tombs, located near modern Verghina, have been excavated in recent decades. One of the unlooted tombs may be that of Philip II, or his illegitimate son Philip III Arrhidaeus. See M. Andronikos, *Vergina: The Royal Tombs and the Ancient City.*

29 The following account is based on Plut. *Pyrr.* 26–34 and Justin 25.

NOTES TO PAGES 33–44

30 D.S. 19.59.3; Plut. *Dem.* 14.2, 37.3; Trogus, *Prol.* 26.

31 Justin 26.1; Paus. 5.5.1; Plut. *Mor.* 251a, 253a.

32 Trogus, *Prol.* 26; Plut. *Arat.* 17.2; for discussion see Hammond and Walbank, *A History of Macedonia*, vol. III, p. 301, Green, *Alexander to Actium*, p. 148, and *CAH* 7², 247.

33 Plut. *Arat.* 17; Polyaen. 4.6.1.

34 Paus. 2.8.4, 7.8.3; Plut. *Arat.* 18.1, 22.3, 23.4; Polyaen. 6.5.

35 No. 23 in E. LeGrand, "Inscriptions de Trezene." A broken statue base containing the words *phrourarchos* ("garrison commander") and *phrour-* (probably "garrison").

36 Polyaen. 5.17; *PHerc.* 1418; D.L. 2.127, 4.29; *Syll.*³ 454, Plut. *Arat.* 34.1.

37 For example, *I.G.* II², 1217, 1280, 1281, 1285; *SEG* III, 122; *SEG* XXV, 153, 155.

38 Not much is left of the city today, but enough foundation stones to confirm its size and the strength of its walls. The earlier archaeological investigation published by F. Staehlin, *et al.*, *Pagasai und Demetrias. Beschreibung der Reste und Stadtgeschichte*, is revised in some particulars by N.D. Papahadjis, "The Palace of Macedonian Kings in Demetrias," and S.C. Bakhuizen, "Renewed Investigation of Goritsa (Thessaly)." Milojcic and Theocharis have published recent work in *Demetrias I.*

39 *I.G.* II², 683, 775, 776, 780, 803; B.D. Meritt, "Athenian Archons 347/6–48/7 BC;" W.B. Dinsmoor, "The Archonship of Pytharatos."

40 Emile Bourguet, *Fouilles de Delphes*, vol. III: Epigraphie, fasc. 1, no. 479; *SEG* II.261; Beloch, *Griechische Geschichte* IV, p. 2, 503; Flacelière, *Les Aitoliens à Delphes. Contribution à l'histoire de la Grèce centrale au IIIe siècle av. J.C.*, pp. 197–198; Heinz Heinen, "Untersuchungen zur hellenistischen Geschichte des 3. Jahrhunderts v. Chr.", pp. 131, 139–141.

41 Polyb. 2.43.9, 2.45.1, 9.34.6, 9.38.9.

42 Ibid.

43 I have argued elsewhere for the date. See Gabbert, "The Anarchic Dating of the Chremonidean War," pp. 230–235, which contains a full bibliography for other possibilities; there is also more recent discussion in Hammond and Walbank, *A History of Macedonia*, vol. III, pp. 278–80, and Green, *Alexander to Actium*, pp. 147–148. The date of the known Athenian archons for the first and last year of the war remains controversial and much auxiliary evidence has been brought into the effort to date this war, some of it not very relevant. In the final analysis, there is equally good reason to place Peithidemos in 268/7 or 265/4, and Antipater in 263/2 or 262/1. I prefer the shorter chronology for the war because if (and this is a big "if") we know all of the major events of the war, they could, and should, happen within a span of two or three years. If the war lasted longer, we must wonder what else was happening, and we have no evidence of anything else. The placement of Peithidemos in 265/4 and Antipater in 263/2 allows the events of this short war to make sense, but it begs explanation of some apparent hostilities referred to in two inscriptions (*I.G.* II², 665 and 666, archons Menekles and Nikias) rather securely dated to 267/6 and 266/5, the two years previous to the official outbreak of the war, if Peithidemos is correctly placed in 265/4. If we knew the proximate causes of the war, it would help. That there were a few incidents prior to the official declaration of war is certainly possible, and perhaps likely. Whatever the proximate causes were which led to a formal declaration of war and a well-planned strategy by Ptolemy Philadelphus, Athens, Sparta, and perhaps others, they probably took some time to unfold.

44 *I.G.* II², 665, lines 8–12; 666, line 18; 667, line 7. These references, among other things, cause many scholars to date the outbreak of the war to an earlier date.

45 D.L. 7.17; Chremonides was probably a decade or so younger than Antigonus.

46 James McCredie, "Fortified Military Camps in Attica", 113; also *SEG* XXIV.154, an inscription honoring the Athenian Epichares for aiding the troops with Patroclus (among other things).

47 This may be the setting for an incident in Polyaenus (4.6.3), where the Megarians doused pigs with pitch and set them on fire; the "flaming pigs" startled the elephants of Antigonus, who thereafter ordered their handlers to keep pigs among the elephants so that they would get used to the sound and smell (that it was the squealing of the animals rather than the fire which disturbed the elephants). The stratagem was a copy of one worked against Pyrrhus by the Romans, probably at Beneventum. In any case, Antigonus managed to deal with it.

48 Paus. 1.1.1 suggests coastal patrols and landing parties ("he ravaged Attica with an army and a fleet"). This sort of action did not require much of a naval force. It is likely that most of Antigonus' ships remained in port.

49 The notion is so widespread that detailed citation is impractical. Some samples: Tarn, *Antigonos Gonatas*, p. 313; M. Cary, *A History of the Greek World 323–146* BC, p. 134; Grace McCurdy, *Hellenistic Queens* p. 120. A useful correction (with additional citation) is offered by Stanley

Burstein, "Arsinoë II Philadelphus: A Revisionist View." The new edition of *CAH* 7² (Walbank), p. 237, adopts a more moderate view.

50 Burstein, "Arsinoë II Philadelphus," p. 205.

51 That Antigonus was building a fleet, see E. Will, *Histoire politique du monde hellenistique*, vol.I pp. 219–221; that Ptolemy was creating a diversion to mask his movements in the Aegean islands, see E.E. Rice, *The Grand Procession of Ptolemy Philadelphus*, p. 191; that Ptolemy was supporting a patriotic/nationalist move by Athens, C. Habicht, *Untersuchungen zur politischen Geschichte Athens im 3. Jahrhunderts v. Chr.*, pp. 95–112. It is more common, and quite understandable, for scholars to write vaguely about this war and its causes, to suggest multiple possible war aims or general preventive and opportunistic motives on the part of Ptolemy.

52 Apollodorus *FGrH* 244, F44 "and it was set forth that all things should be decided by one [man]." There is no evidence for any "epistates" or overseer appointed by and reporting to Antigonus, not in this case nor anywhere else in Greece. Rather, the "one" referred to was Antigonus himself. This fragment is just that, a fragment without context, and is a secondary or even tertiary source providing vague and rather generalized information from an original source unknown to us.

53 Eusebius, *Chronicon*, enters "Antigonus Atheniensibus rursus dedit libertatem" for the year 255.

54 See Hammond and Walbank, *A History of Macedonia*, vol. III, p. 292 and Appendix 4, "The Date of the Battles of Cos and Andros," pp. 587–600.

NOTES TO PAGES 54–58

55 For full discussion of the festivals, see Hammond and Walbank, *A History of Macedonia*, vol. III, pp. 598–599, and Gary Reger, "The Date of the Battle of Kos," p. 158 and notes.

56 The earlier action of Craterus was discussed in Chapter 5, Ameinias in Chapter 3. For the revolt of Alexander, the major source is Plutarch's life of *Aratus*, 17. Trogus, *Prol.* 26 offers some help, and Suidas, *s.v. Euphorion* identifies Alexander as "king" of "Euboea," and a decree of Eretria (*I.G.* 9, 212) refers to "Alexander the king."

57 Trogus, *Prol.* 27, "Antigonus Andro proelio navali Oprona vicerit;" Plut. *Pelopidas* 2.4. See A.N. Oikonomides, "Opron and the Sea-Battle of Andros," pp. 151–152 and for a recent full discussion, see Hammond, *Macedonia* vol. III, pp. 303–306 and Appendix IV, "The Date of the Battles of Cos and Andros," pp. 587–600.

58 The deities honored are unusual at Delos and therefore these foundations are probably based on a specific event, such as a naval victory: Kostas Buraselis, *Das hellenistische Makedonien und die Agäis*, pp. 144–145.

59 Plut. *Arat.* 18–23; Polyaen. 6.5; Paus. 2.8.4, 7.8.3; Athenaeus 162d; Trogus, *Prol.* 26. In some versions Persaios escaped the carnage.

60 Plut. *Arat.* 24.3; Paus. 2.8.5; Polyb. 2.43.4.

61 Polyb. 2.43.9, 2.45.1, 9.34.6, 9.38.9.

62 Hammond, *Macedonia*, vol. III, p. 313, n. 6.

NOTES TO PAGES 59–67

63 Ernst Badian, "A King's Notebooks," p. 198.

64 R.M. Errington, "The Nature of the Macedonian State under the Monarchy," pp. 77–133, *passim*. Errington rightly considers an informal consensus of support, especially by the nobility, to have been the most important political basis for the royal exercise of power.

65 Rudolf Herzog and Gunther Klaffenbach, *Asylieurkunden aus Kos*, Nos. 6 and 7.

66 Hammond, *Macedonia*, vol. III, locates an Antigoneia in Epirus on the map, Fig. 8 (p. 153), and another on the Axius river in Macedonia on the map, Fig. 3 (p. 33), which he indicates was *probably* founded by Antigonus Gonatas (p. 268); both are mentioned in the narrative of events much later than Antigonus (pp. 333, 423, 526) and may have been founded by Antigonus Doson or by Demetrius II and named after his father. The *Antigoneia* in Epirus was probably founded by Pyrrhus in 295 and named after his wife Antigone.

67 E. Van't Dack, "Recherches sur les institutions de village en Egypte ptolemaique," esp. pp. 21–22. Most *epistatai* are minor local officials, and none is earlier than 223 BC.

68 F. Granier, *Die Makedonische Heeresversammlung: ein Beitrag zum antiken staatsrecht* and H. Bengtson, *Die Strategie in der hellenistischen Zeit* have made an ambitious attempt to define Antigonid officials, but the reality remains ambiguous.

69 Edward N. Luttwak, *The Grand Strategy of the Roman Empire*.

70 Walter Lacquer, "Europe: The Specter of Finlandization," pp. 37–41.

NOTES TO PAGES 68–72

71 Tarn, op cit., p. 174 discusses his image as Pan on coins, but see C.F. Leon, "Antigonos Gonatas Rediscovered," pp. 21–25, for a detailed discussion of a recently discovered bronze bust in a private collection and its relationship (or lack of it) to the coin portraiture. Plutarch's comment on the ugliness of Antigonus may have been based on the images on the coins; we don't know what other representations of Antigonus may have existed.

72 Leon, ibid., p. 22. The illustration does not look very terrifying to this observer.

73 F. Staehlin *et al.*, *Pagasai und Demetrias. Beschreibung der Reste und Stadtgeschichte*; V. Milojcic and D. Theocharis, *Demetrias I*; N.D. Papahadjis, "The Palace of Macedonian Kings in Demetrias"; Ph. Petsas, "Pella, the Capital of the Macedonian Kings"; Manolis Andronicos, *Vergina: The Royal Tombs and Other Antiquities*, and *Vergina: The Royal Tombs and the Ancient City*.

74 Tarn, op. cit., Chapter 8, pp. 223–256.

75 The 13th Rock Edict, *c.* 256 BC: J. Bloch, *Les Inscriptions d'Asoka*; E. Yamauchi, "Hellenistic Bactria and Buddhism," p. 9. The mission of these envoys is not certain, and there is no record of their arrival at any of their western destinations, nor of anything accomplished.

BIBLIOGRAPHY

ANCIENT SOURCES

Sources are preceded by abbreviations used in the text if different from those used in Liddell-Scott-Jones *Greek–English Lexicon*, 9th edn, Oxford University Press, 1973.

Aelian   Claudii Aeliani. *Varia Historia*. Ed. Merwin Dilts. Leipzig (1974).

Athenaeus   *Dipnosophistae*. Ed. G. Kaibel. 3 vols. Leipzig (1886–90).

D.S.   Diodorus Siculus. *Bibliotheca Historica*. Ed. F. Vogel and C.T. Fisher. 6 vols. Leipzig (1888–1906).

D.L.   Diogenes Laertius. *Vitae Philosophorum*. Ed. H.S. Long. 2 vols. Oxford (1964).

Epicurus   In C. Diano. *Lettere di Epicuro e dei suoi*. Florence (1946).

Eusebius   *Eusebi Chronicorum Libri duo*. Ed. Alfred Schoene. Berlin (1866–75).

Frontinus   Sextus Julius Frontinus. *Strategematon*. Ed. G. Gunderman. Leipzig (1888).

FGrH   other fragmentary writers in F. Jacoby, ed., *Die Fragmente der grieschischen Historiker*. Berlin and Leiden (1923–57).

Justin   Marcus Junius Justinus. *Epitoma Historiarum Philippicarum Pompei Trogi*, with the Prologues of Pompeius Trogus, Ed. Otto Seel. Leipzig (1935).

Livy   Titus Livius. *Ab urbe condita libri*. Ed. W. Weissenborn and M. Mueller. 4 vols. Stuttgart (1966).

Paus.   Pausanias. *Descriptio Graeciae*. Ed. Maria Helena Roch-Pereira. 2 vols. Leipzig (1973).

Pliny   Plinius. Historia Naturalis. Ed. C. Mayhoff. 5 vols. Leipzig (1892–1909).

Plut.   Plutarchus. *Mor.* = *Moralia*. Ed. C. Hubert *et al.* 7 vols. Leipzig (1925–78); from the *Vitae Parallelae*. Ed. K. Ziegler. 3 vols. Leipzig (1960–71): biographies of Aratus (*Arat.*), Demetrius (*Dem.*), Pelopidas (*Pelop.*) and Pyrrhus (*Pyrr.*).

Polyaen.   Polyaenus. *Strategemata*. Ed. E. Woelfflin *et al.* Stuttgart (1970).

Polyb.   Polybius. *Historiae*. Ed. L. Dindorf and T. Buettner-Wobst. 5 vols. Stuttgart (1962–3).
Sextus   *Adversus Mathematicos: I. Adversus Grammaticos*. Ed. H.
Empiricus   Mutschmann. Leipzig (1912); rev. J. Mau and K. Janacek (1954).
Stobaeus,   *Anthologium*. Ed. A. Meinike. 3 vols. Leipzig (1855).
Joannes
Strabo   *Geographica*. Ed. A. Meinike. 3 vols. Leipzig (1877).
Suidas   *Suidae Lexicon*. Ed. A. Adler. 4 vols. Leipzig (1928–35).

EPIGRAPHICAL PUBLICATIONS

Inscriptiones *Consilio et Auctoritate Academiae Litterarum Borussicae*
Graecae   *Editae*. 15 vols. Berlin (1873–) (editio altera, 1913–), particularly the following volumes:
I.G. II²   *Inscriptiones Atticae Euclidis anno posteriores*. Ed. J. Kirchner. 4 parts (1913–40).
I.G. IX, part 2 *Inscriptiones Thessaliae*. Ed. O. Kern (1908).
I.G. X, part 2, *Inscriptiones Thessalonicae et viciniae*. Ed. C. Edson (1972).
fasc. 1
SEG   *Supplementum Epigraphicum Graecum*. Ed. P. Roussel *et al.* Leiden (1923–).
*Syll.*³   *Sylloge Inscriptionum Graecarum*. 3rd edn. Ed. W. Dittenberger, 5 vols. Leipzig (1915–24).

PAPYROLOGICAL PUBLICATIONS

P Herc.   [Herculaneum Papyri] in A. Vogliano, "Nuovi Testi Storici," *Rivista di Filologia e di Istruzione Classica* 54 (1926), 310–331.
P.Oxy.   *Oxyrhnchus Papyri*. Ed. B.P. Grenfell and A.S. Hunt. London (1898).

ABBREVIATIONS

AJAH   *American Journal of Ancient History*
AJP   *American Journal of Philology*
AncW   *The Ancient World*
ANSMN   *American Numismatic Society Museum Notes*
BCH   *Bulletin de Correspondence Hellenique*
CAH   *Cambridge Ancient History*
CAH 7²   *Cambridge Ancient History*, vol. 7, 2nd edn
CJ   *Classical Journal*
CPh   *Classical Philology*
CQ   *Classical Quarterly*
GRBS   *Greek, Roman and Byzantine Studies*
HSCP   *Harvard Studies in Classical Philology*
REG   *Revue des Etudes Grecques*
ZPE   *Zeitschrift für Papyrusforschung und Epigraphie*

SECONDARY SOURCES

Adams, W. Lindsay and Eugene N. Borza, eds *Philip II, Alexander the Great and the Macedonian Heritage*. Washington, D.C. (1982).

Adams, W.L. "Antipater and Cassander: Generalship on Restricted Resources in the Fourth Century," *AncW* 10 (1984), 79–88.

Adcock, F. "Greek and Macedonian Kingship," *Proceedings of the British Academy*, no. 39, 1953.

Alexander, John A. "Cassandreia During the Macedonian Period: An Epigraphical Commentary," in *Ancient Macedonia*. Papers read at the First International Symposium held in Thessaloniki, 26–29 August 1968, pp. 127–46. Basil Laourdas and Ch. Makaronas, eds. Thessaloniki: Institute for Balkan Studies (1970).

Andronicos, Manolis *Vergina: The Royal Tombs and Other Antiquities*. Athens (1984).

—— *Vergina: The Royal Tombs and the Ancient City*. Athens (1987).

Anson, Edward M. "Macedonia's Alleged Constitutionalism," *CJ* 80 (1985), 303–316.

Arrighetti, G., ed. *Epicuro Opere*. Turin (1960).

Badian, Ernst "A King's Notebooks," *HSCP* 72 (1967), 183–204.

Bakhuizen, S.C. "Renewed Investigation of Goritsa (Thessaly)," *Athens Annals of Archaeology* 5 (1972), 485–495.

Beloch, Julius *Griechische Geschichte*. 2nd edn, 4 vols. Berlin (1912–27).

—— "Mithres," *Rivista di Filologia e di lstruzione Classica* 54 (1926), 331–335.

Bengston, H. *Die Strategie in der hellenistischen Zeit*. 3 vols. Munich (1937–52).

—— *Die Diadochen: Die Nachfolger Alexanders des Grossen*. Munich (1987).

Billows, Richard A. *Antigonos the One-Eyed and the Creation of the Hellenistic State*. California (1990).

Bloch, J. *Les Inscriptions d'Asoka*. Paris (1950).

Bourguet, Emile *Fouilles de Delphes*. Vol. III: Epigraphie. fasc. 1: Inscriptions de l'entrée du sanctuaire au trésor des Athéniens. Paris (1929).

Brown, E.L. "Antigonus Surnamed Gonatas," in *Arktouros: Hellenic Studies Presented to Bernard M.W. Knox* on the occasion of his 65th birthday, pp. 299–307. G.W. Bowersock, Walter Burkert, and Michael C.J. Putnam, eds. New York (1979).

Buraselis, Kostas *Das hellenistische Makedonien und die Ägäis: Forschungen zur Politik des Kassandros und der drei ersten Antigoniden (Antigonos Monopthalmos, Demetrios Poliorketes und Antigonos Gonatas) im Ägäischen Meer und in Westkleinasien*. Münchener Beiträge zur Papyrusforschung und antiken Rechtsgeschichte, 73. Munich (1982).

Burstein, Stanley M. "Bithys, Son of Cleon from Lysimacheia: A Reconsideration of the Date and Significance of *IG* II², 808," *California Studies in Classical Antiquity* 12 (1979), 39–50.

—— "Arsinoë II Philadelphus: A Revisionist View," in *Philip II, Alexander the Great and the Macedonian Heritage*, W.L. Adams and E.N. Borza, eds. Washington, D.C. (1982), pp. 197–212.

Cary, M. *A History of the Greek World 323–146* BC. 2nd edn. London, (1951).

Carney, E.D. "Arsinoë Before She Was Philadelphus," *Ancient History Bulletin* 8 (1994), 123–131.

Chambers, M. "The First Regnal Year of Antigonus Gonatas," *AJP* 75 (1954), 385–394.

Ciocolo, Sandrina "Enigmi dell'Noos: Antigono II Gonata in Plutarco," *Studi Ellenistici* 48 (1984), 135–190.

Cohen, G.M. "The Marriage of Lysimachus and Nicaea," *Historia* 22 (1973), 354–356.

—— "The Diadochoi and the New Monarchies," *Athenaeum* 52 (1974), 177–179.

Diano, C. *Lettere di Epicuro e dei suoi.* Florence (1946).

Dinsmoor, W.B. "The Archonship of Pytharatos," *Hesperia* 23 (1954), 284–316.

Dow, Sterling "Thrasyphon Hierokleidou Xypetaion," *GRBS* 20 (1979), 331–345.

Edson, Ch. F. "The Antigonids, Heracles and Beroea," *Harvard Classical Studies* XLV (1934), 213–246.

Errington, R. Malcolm. "The Nature of the Macedonian State Under the Monarchy," *Chiron* 8 (1978), 77–133.

—— *A History of Macedonia.* Trans. Catharine Errington. California (1990).

Ferguson, W.S. *Hellenistic Athens.* London (1911).

—— "Lachares and Demetrius Poliorcetes," *CPh* (1929), 1–31.

—— "Polyeuktos and the Soteria," *ASP* 55 (1934), 318–336.

Fine, J.V.A. "The Antigonids," *The Greek Political Experience: Studies in Honor of W. K. Prentice.* Princeton (1941).

Flacelière, R. *Les Aitoliens à Delphes. Contribution à l'histoire de la Grèce centrale au IIIe siècle av. J.C.* Bibliographie des Ecoles françaises d'Athènes et de Rome CXLIII, Paris (1937).

Foraboschi, Daniele *Onomasticon Alterum Papyrologicum. Supplemento al Namenbuch di F. Preisigke.* Milan (1967).

Gabbert, J. "Pragmatic Democracy in Hellenistic Athens," *AncW* 13 (1986), 29–33.

—— "The Anarchic Dating of the Chremonidean War," *CJ* 82 (1987), 230–235.

—— "The Career of Olympiodorus of Athens (ca.340–270 BC)", *AncW* 27 (1996), 59–66.

Gauthier, Philippe "La Réunification d'Athènes en 281 et les deux archontes Nicias," *REG* 92 (1979), 348–399.

Geyer, F. "Euboia in den Wirren der Diadochenzeit," *Philologus* 39 (1930), 175–191.

Golan, David "Aratus' Policy Between Sicyon and Argos: An Attempt at Greek Unity," *R. storia antichita* 3 (1973), 59–70.

Granier, Friedrich *Die Makedonische Heeresversammlung: ein Beitrag zum antiken staatsrecht. Münchener Beiträge zur Papyrusforschung und antiken rechtsgeschichte* vol. 13. Munich (1931).

Green, Peter *Alexander to Actium: The Historical Evolution of the Hellenistic Age.* California (1990).

Griffith, G.T. *The Mercenaries of the Hellenistic World.* Cambridge (1935).

Gruen, E.S. *The Hellenistic World and the Romans.* 2 vols. California (1984).

Habicht, Christian *Untersuchungen zur politischen Geschichte Athens im 3. Jahrhundert v. Chr. Vestigia, Beiträge zur Alten Geschichte,* 30. Munich (1979).

Hammond, N.G.L. *The Macedonian State: Origins, Institutions, and History.* Oxford (1990).

—— and F. W. Walbank *A History of Macedonia, vol. III: 336–167* BC. Oxford, (1988).

Heinen, Heinz "Untersuchungen zur hellenistischen Geschichte des 3. Jahrhunderts v. Chr," *Historia Einzelschriften,* vol. 20, Wiesbaden (1972).

Herzog, Rudolf and Gunther Klaffenbach *Asylieurkunden aus Kos.* Abhandlungen der Deutschen Akademie der Wissenschaften zu Berlin Nos. 6 and 7 (1952).

Hunt, A.S., ed. *The Oxyrhynchus Papyri. Part XVII.* London: Egypt Exploration Society (1927).

Jacoby, Felix, ed. *Die Fragmente der griechischen Historiker.* Berlin and Leiden (1923–1957).

Jones, Christopher P. "The Decree of Ilion in Honor of a King Antiochus," *GRBS* 34 (1993), 73–92.

Klose, Peter *Die völkerrechtliche Ordnung der hellenistischen Staatenwelt in der Zeit von 280 bis 168 v. Chr. Münchener Beiträge zur Papyrusforschung und antiken Rechtsgeschichte* vol. 64. Munich (1972).

Lacquer, Walter "Europe: The Specter of Finlandization," *Commentary* (December, 1977), 37–41.

Larson, J.A.O. *Greek Federal States.* Oxford (1968).

LeBohec, Sylvie. "Les épistates des rois antigonides," *Ktema* 11 (1986), 281–288.

LeGrand, E. "Inscriptions de Trezene," *BCH* 17 (1893), 84–121.

Leon, C.F. "Antigonos Gonatas Rediscovered," *AncW* 20 (1989), 21–25.

Luttwak, Edward N. *The Grand Strategy of the Roman Empire.* Baltimore (1976).

McCredie, James R. "Fortified Military Camps in Attica," *Hesperia,* Supp. XI, (1966).

McCurdy, Grace *Hellenistic Queens.* Baltimore (1932).

Mandel, J. "A propos d'une dynastie de tyrans à Argos (III siècle avant J.C.)," *Athenaeum* 57 (1979), 293–307.

Manni, E. "Due battaglie di Andro?" *Athenaeum* 30 (1952), 182–190.

—— "Note di Cronologia Ellenistica, X," *Athenaeum* 40 (1962), 315–324.

—— "Note di Cronologia Ellenistica, XI," *Athenaeum* 46 (1968), 112–121.

Mathisen, Ralph W. "Memnon of Herakleia on Antigonos Gonatas, 280–277 BC," *AncW* 1, (1978), 71–74.

—— "Antigonus Gonatas and the Silver Coinages of Macedonia circa 280–270 BC," *ANSMN* 26 (1981), 79–124.

Meritt, Benjamin D. "Athenian Archons 347/6–48/7 BC," *Historia* 26 (1977), 161–191.

Milojcic, V. "Bericht über die deutschen archäologischen Ausgrabungen in Thessalien, 1973," *Archaiologika Analekta eks Athēnon* 7 (1974), 43–75.

—— and D. Theocharis. *Demetrias I. Beiträge zur ur-und frühgeschichtlichen Archäologie des Mittelmeer-Kulturraumes,* vol 12. Bonn (1976).

Momigliano, A. "A New Date for the Battle of Andros? A Discussion," *CQ* 44 (1950), 107–116.

Nachtergael, G. *Les Galates en Grèce et les Soteria de Delphes. Recherches d'histoire et d'épigraphie hellénistiques.* Brussels (1977).

Oikonomides, A.N. "Opron and the Sea-Battle of Andros," *Zeitschrift Für Papyrologie Und Epigraphik* 56 (1984), 151–152.

Orth, Wolfgang *Königlicher Machtanspruch und städtische Freiheit: Untersuchungen zu den politischen Beziehungen zwischen den ersten Seleukidenherrschen (Seleukos I, Antiochos I, Antiochos II) und den Städten des westlichen Kleinasiens.* (Münchener Beiträge zur Papyrusforschung und Antiken Rechtsgeschichte, number 71). Munich (1977).

Osborne, Michael J. "Kallias, Phaidros, and the Revolt of Athens in 287 BC," *ZPE* 35 (1979), 181–194.

—— "The Chronology of Athens in the Mid-Third Century, BC," *ZPE* 78 (1989), 209–242.

Panagos, Ch. Th. *Le Pirée.* Trans. Pierre Gerardat. Athens (1968).

Papahadjis, N.D. "The Palace of Macedonian Kings in Demetrias," *Thessalika* I (1958), 16–26. (in Greek with resumé in English)

Petrakos, Basil "Neai Pegai peri tou Chremonideiou polemou," *Archaiologikon Deltikon* 22A (1967), 38–52.

Petsas, Ph. M. "Pella, the Capital of the Macedonian Kings," *Athene*, 23,3 (1962), 13–16; 23,4, 71–73.

Porter, W.H. "Aratus of Sicyon and King Antigonos Gonatas," *Hermathena* 45 (1930), 293–311.

Pouilloux, Jean *La forteresse de Rhamnonte.* Paris (1954).

Reger, Gary "The Date of the Battle of Kos," *AJAH* 10 (1985) [1993], 155–177.

Rice, E.E. *The Grand Procession of Ptolemy Philadelphia.* Oxford (1983).

Robert, J. and Robert, L. "Bulletin Epigraphique," *REG* 64 (1951), 119–126.

de Sanctis, Gaetano "Il dominio macedonico nel Pireo," *Rivista di Filologia e d'istruzione classica* (1927) 480–500.

Sarikakis, Theodore Chr. "The Athenian Generals in Hellenistic Times," (in Greek), *Athena* 57 (1953), 242–304.

Sartori, F. "L'Ateniese Cremonide alla corte dei Tolomei," *Ricerche Storiche ed economiche in memoria di Corrado Barbagallo.* 3 vols. Naples (1970), vol. 1, 445–456.

Schoch, Paul *Prosopographie der militärischen und politischen Funktionäre im hellenistischen Makedonien (323–168 v. Chr.) Diss.* Basel (1919).

Seibert, J. *Historische Beiträge zu den dynastischen Verbindungen in hellenistischer Zeit. Historia Einzelschriften* vol. 40, Wiesbaden (1967), 129–131.

Shear T. Leslie, Jr. "Kallias of Sphettos and the Revolt of Athens in 286 BC," *Hesperia* Suppl. XVII, Princeton (1978).

Simpson, R.M. "Antigonus the One-Eyed and the Greeks," *Historia* 8 (1959), 385–409.

Staehlin, F. *et. al. Pagasai und Demetrias. Beschreibung der Reste und Stadtgeschichte.* Berlin (1934).

Tarn, W.W. *Antigonos Gonatas.* Oxford (1913).

—— *The Cambridge Ancient History*, vol. VII: *The Hellenistic Monarchies and the Rise of Rome*. Cambridge (1928). III "The New Hellenistic Kingdoms," pp. 75–108; VI "Macedonia and Greece," pp. 197–223; and XXII "The Struggle of Egypt Against Syria and Macedonia," pp. 699–731.

Van't Dack, E. "Recherches sur les institutions de village en Egypte ptolemaique," *Studia Hellenistica 7, Ptolemaica*, Louvain (1951), 5–38.

Walbank, F.W. *Aratos of Sicyon*. London (1933).

—— *A Historical Commentary on Polybius*. 2 vols. Oxford (1957–67).

—— "Sea-power and the Antigonids," in *Philip II, Alexander the Great and the Macedonian Heritage*, W. Lindsay Adams and Eugene N. Borza, eds. Washington, D.C. (1982), pp. 213–236.

—— *et al. The Cambridge Ancient History*. 2nd edn, vol. VII, Part 1, "The Hellenistic World." Cambridge (1984).

Will, Edouard. *Histoire politique du monde hellénistique (323–30 av. J.C.)*. 2 vols., 2nd edn (1979–82).

Yamauchi, E. "Hellenistic Bactria and Buddhism," *Humanitas* 18.3 (1995), 5–10.

INDEX